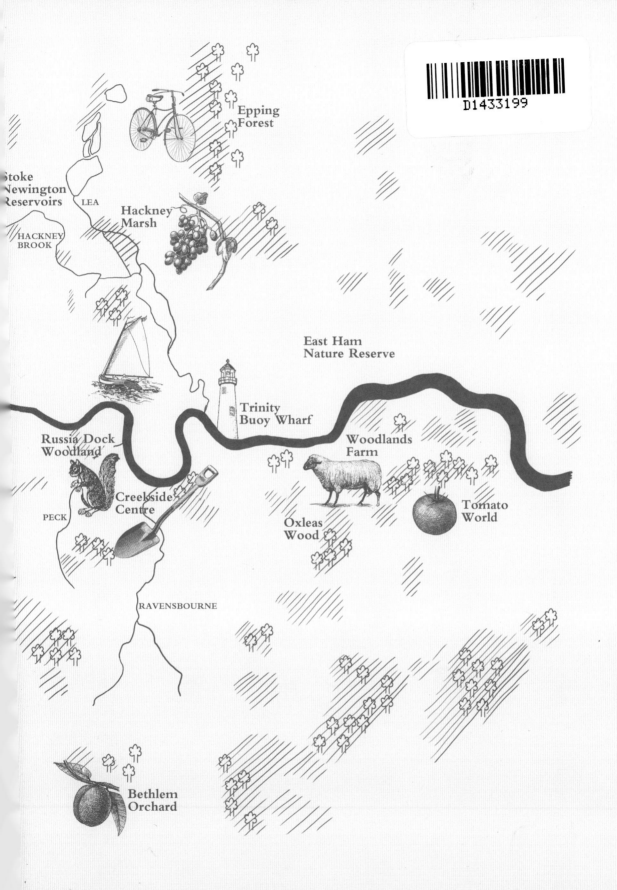

Epping
Forest

Stoke
Newington
Reservoirs

LEA

HACKNEY
BROOK

Hackney
Marsh

East Ham
Nature Reserve

Trinity
Buoy Wharf

Russia Dock
Woodland

Woodlands
Farm

Creekside
Centre

PECK

Oxleas
Wood

Tomato
World

RAVENSBOURNE

Bethlem
Orchard

LOST *in* LONDON

Lucy Scott & Tina Smith

Contents

Natural city

Life on the water

Journeys through trees

Urban farmer's handbook

It is truly incredible just how many opportunities there are in London to put on a pair of walking boots and make contact with real earth.

They are opportunities that are very easy to forget. As Londoners, we are so used to navigating the city according to its manufactured environment and networks – using tube maps, bus routes and postcard landmarks as tools – that the idea that this city has any natural landscape worth thinking about is hard to fathom.

For the past few years, we have been exploring and celebrating the green within the grey through our seasonal magazine *Lost in London*, to show city dwellers that there is a simpler, slower life to be had. But we wanted to take that idea of the city as a natural place to a deeper level. With this book we wanted to fade out the buildings just that little bit more.

So we started out with a map of London that didn't include the M25, a web of A roads or suburbs. One that instead revealed its heathlands and meadows, ancient woodlands and pastures, chalk streams, creeks, and marshes. That showed a landscape of clay, sandstone or loam, and waters that can be fast flowing, tidal or meandering. A map that used names like the Lee Valley, the North Downs and the Ruislip Plateau.

This book is a collection of journeys along those natural contours. Journeys that might have begun on a tube train but ended at some other place entirely: under a canopy of trees, exploring a riverbed at low tide, or navigating a heath in the depths of night.

It is a reflection of the stories of the people and wildlife we encountered while we were there, and an attempt to record and celebrate lives lived in the spaces in between. Above all, it is an attempt to capture something of the rhythms and mysteries of a landscape, and bring them here.

It's an ode to London's landscape.

Lucy Scott & Tina Smith

PHOTOGRAPHY: LEE HICKMAN

Natural
city

Wet and wild

Words by Lucy Scott. Illustrations by Karolin Schnoor

On the news that morning, they had told Londoners to write off June. June was going to be wet. Sure enough, it had been another watery day, and the world on the other side of my rain-streaked window was dreary.

As I worked at my desk in one of my winter jumpers, my neighbours were outdoors, defiantly honouring the summer of which the city was being robbed. They clinked beer bottles with friends under the shelter of a bright blue tarpaulin, hastily erected over their new decking, and there they stayed all afternoon, as the roof became ever more saggy with a deep puddle of the water, watching the smoke from their barbecue trying to make an effort. I watched it too, the prospect of heading across London for a wildflower tour of Lewisham fast losing appeal.

I had called the Creekside Centre a couple of times that afternoon, in the hope that it had been called off. No such luck. Nick, my guide, would be waiting for me outside Grove Park Station at 6pm.

As I arrive, my wet-weather blues lift. Nick is animated, caught up in a debate with fellow botanical enthusiast Chris, who had come along for the ride. Nick is peering through a magnifying glass, and they are scrutinising a leafy and limey-green stalk that he has picked up on the curbside on the way over. I move closer to examine its tiny, star-shaped yellow flowers, bright against the blurred backdrop of the high street, as a 126 to Bromley South roars past, sending a knee-high spray of water onto the curb.

I guess it's a kind of Euphorbia. "It looks like it but it isn't." So much for *Gardeners' World*, I think. "See those leaves perforated by the stem?" he asks, pointing. "They're characteristic of the thorow-wax. I just picked it off the platform display but I've never seen one growing wild in London," he enthuses, zipping the specimen away in his pac-a-mac. At home later, equally curious, I look up what Nick thought he'd seen, and discover it in Richard Mabey's *Flora Britannica*. The entry is so uncanny, I have to read it twice.

Thorow-wax is now probably extinct as a wild plant in Britain. Its only recent appearance was recorded in 1990, in north London, after the plant had made its way into the wreath on a new grave in St Pancras and Islington cemetery, weaving itself around the formal arrangement of chrysanthemums, irises and carnations. "The large tufts of a yellow green colour ... glowed with astonishing vividness on an overcast day," said *Britannica*. It may have not been wild but, like a miracle, the thorow-wax had presented itself to us in similar circumstances. Although,

by then I had already learned that wildflowers are nothing if not miraculous, and those in London especially so.

We cross the road and turn into a street of brownish-grey terraced houses, as rain drives rain. The walk had been billed as a Three Rivers Crossing, so I had anticipated we would be checking out the flora growing bank-side along the Ravensbourne, Quaggy and Pool that flow from south-east London to the large U-bend in the Thames made famous by *Eastenders*.

Between a parked silver car and someone's perfectly rectangular hedge, the three of us crouch down on the pavement as Nick points one by one to the shoots sprouting from cracks in the patchwork of slabs.

"Cut-leaved cranesbill. Petty spurge. Common ragwort. Groundsel – that's related to ragwort – and just over there is Oxford ragwort. Three common ragworts of London, all within just a couple of metres.

"Over there, look, knotgrass – an abundant plant of bare places, gardens and cultivated ground," he continues, as we take a few steps further along the street. "Then over here we have bellflower. It's from southern Europe but there are large colonies of it in south-east London; the wind-blown seeds establish easily on bare patches of chalk. Much of the soil in this area has some chalk like characteristics because of the amount of mortar and cement used in urban areas."

He eases the bottom of the hedge away from the floor to reveal the line of plants growing in the seam between the slabs and the garden. Wild fennel, introduced by the Romans as a medicinal and culinary herb. Smooth sow thistle, a common annual of waste, cultivated and disturbed ground, whose seeds change colour from silver to gold as they ripen. And wall lettuce, a relative of the lettuces we eat. "There is such a huge diversity of plants growing on the edges of pavements in London, and there are hundreds of flowers that have escaped from people's gardens that are now living wild. Paving slabs are lying on sand or soil, so as long as a plant can get the roots through, they're away."

It was in the early 1980s that London wildflower enthusiasts such as Nick uncovered their first real evidence that the city's population was as diverse as they had suspected. In 1983, London botanist Rodney Burton published the *Flora of the London Area* – a work, 18 years in the making, that listed the names of 2,000 species of wild plants within a 20-mile radius of the City of London.

Burton's findings couldn't have been better timed; wildflowers were revelling in some post-industrial halcyon days. Back then, Nick was working shifts on the Underground at Rotherhithe Station. "The city was so wild you wouldn't believe it. There was this huge release of land after the closure of the dockyards. After my shifts, I used to explore places like the Surrey Docks. There were skylarks breeding and these huge areas of wasteland were just full of flowers. I didn't know much about flowers, so I bought a second-hand book and hunted around trying to name what I saw, there and around the capital. It was the beginning of a huge journey of discovery."

Thirty years on, Nick is now taking part in a sequel to Burton's work, a decade-long project led by Dr Mark Spencer of the Natural History Museum. The project, called Flora of London, has enlisted the help of volunteers and botanists to comb every inch of the city, season after season, to record the detailed comings and goings of the flora that inhabit it.

Nick is a recorder for TQ37, a 10 kilometre square patch of land that takes in the Houses of Parliament and the O2 Dome. Repeated visits are necessary, to catch the briefest of appearances. As Nick explains: "I was up near Bricklayers Arms roundabout the other day and noticed elegant clarkia in flower – a plant typically found in the hills of Yosemite – growing on a pavement. It will be there for a short time and then it will be gone. It will have grown in someone's garden, produced seed, and, amazingly, one of them has got into the cracks and got going. The chances of so many of these plants taking root are so infinitesimally small that each one of them is a small miracle happening before your eyes."

In the same way that the people of a city are constantly coming and going, so too are wildflowers; their populations are in constant flux. The research is still in its early stages, but botanists like Mark Spencer know that many more species have found their way on the wind, onto the streets, roadsides, railways and waterways, since Burton compiled his list all those years ago.

London's plant diversity is partly as a result of the vast number of species being grown in gardens. But it is also down to the "heat island effect": London is a few degrees warmer than the countryside, which enables an increasing number of species to thrive in the crevices of the built environment. "There is so much here that most of the wildflower books don't cover it all. So you need to learn some things for yourself," says Nick. "Sometimes it takes years to find out."

But although species such as London rocket have

been here for hundreds of years and are still thriving, the Natural History Museum believes our native flora are ever-decreasing. And although some non-natives such as Oxford ragwort and broad-leaved everlasting-pea cause no harm to the landscape, some, such as Japanese knotweed and buddleia, are invasive. They are able to overpower all other species around them, changing the soil chemistry and capturing pollinators and space. Left unchecked, they can take over completely.

Mark had told me weeks earlier that London has lost hundreds of species in recent years, including marsh sow-thistle, which once grew alongside the Thames, and now teeters on the brink of extinction. Mark has been working with local enthusiasts to establish a population of it at Thames Road Wetland by planting individuals grown from seed collected at Crayford Marshes. Although the reasons for the loss of natives are complex, Mark says a big contributing factor is poor management of our green spaces.

"London has a lot of green space but the critical thing is the quality of it. It is important we manage areas well to maintain the diversity of an area," he says.

Nick, Chris and I pause at a small bridge over the Ravensbourne and look down at the rampant tangle of vegetation colonising the water. A few years ago, this stretch of river was contained in a concrete tunnel, until a restoration project opened it up and turned it into a naturalistic area. With swords of yellow flag iris rising up from the water and the deep pink flowers of common mallow dotted on the banks, it looks healthy enough to me. But Nick is worried about its future. "See the masses of nettles, bindweed and brambles? These plants are enormously powerful. They take off and they take over."

Later, we make our way through the ancient woodland of Beckenham Place Park, the leaves of oaks and hornbeam breaking the water's fall from the sky. We emerge onto the golf course – which the rain has emptied of golfers – and head up towards the blackened ruins of a pair of stable blocks. Set on fire last summer, they have been left to nature ever since. In the old kitchen gardens in front, where rows of vegetables may once have grown within neat borders, sow-thistle now dominates.

I walk around to the back of one of the houses and, through the sliver of space between the "keep out" signs, I try to peer into its empty heart. Just visible are row upon row of tall green things, standing in the rain. Sentinels amid the debris, ready to charge forth into battle. Ready, when the time comes, to release their spirits into the air.

> The chances of so many of these plants taking root are so infinitesimally small that each one of them is a small miracle

To dye for

Words by Helen Babbs. Photography by Rachel Warne

When dyer and designer Katelyn Toth Fejel first moved to Hackney Wick, she didn't like it much. She was craving something wild, and the area didn't seem to offer that. Then while walking alone one day she discovered the marshes when she ventured off her usual path. Suddenly she was lost in the undergrowth, surrounded by a rich knot of plant life. She had, at last, found herself a local patch.

I meet Katelyn at her warehouse home as she packs up kit for a foraging session. We're going to hunt for dye plants in a clump of woodland off the River Lee towpath. She leads the way by bicycle, negotiating her trailer through messy roadworks and over bone-shaking cobbles, past the scars of the Olympics and beneath busy road bridges. Her handmade white dress billows about her like a sail.

It's not long before we disappear down a rough path, made into a romantic tunnel by trees that bend over to meet in the middle. It's the first day of sun after weeks of rain, and the wood is deep green, lush and muddy. It turns out that ten minutes from Hackney Wick Station wilderness reigns.

"I like foraging locally because I can monitor my patch. It's about paying attention," says Katelyn. "You have to be really responsible. I was taught by a Native American basket weaver that you should never take more than a tenth of what you find. And I would never take anything uncommon, like lichen or mushrooms, even though they make really great dyes."

Katelyn is part of the Permacouture Institute and organises Dinners To Dye For, which involve natural dyeing workshops paired with shared meals using plants, nuts and berries that have been foraged locally. Many natural dyes are edible, which means you can use your pickings to both colour your cloth and make your meal. The institute was founded in America by Sasha Duerr, and Katelyn has brought it to Britain.

"We're inspired by permaculture," she explains. "I approach fashion as if it were an ecology, an ecosystem. People are starting to think about food provenance more and more, but we don't really think about fashion provenance yet. We can use people's connection with food as a way in. Our workshops are a sensory experience

and can turn something banal like an onion skin into something magical."

Katelyn pulls on thick gloves and starts harvesting bundles of nettles and stuffing them into a huge cooking pot, where they will later be boiled in water to make a green/yellow dye. "Nettle is a food, a fibre and a dye. And there's so much of it. I'm thinking about overlooked local resources and trying to encourage eco-literacy." She grabs a trowel and heads into the bushes to find a dock root, before returning with an enormous specimen.

"You can make lots of different pinks with dock root by adding an alkaline like baking soda to the dye. If you added something acidic you'd get yellow. There's a huge variety to be had from one plant. You also get drastically different colours depending on the natural conditions, like the soil. In the same way that there are distinctive wine regions, there are colour regions too."

The preparation depends on what you're dealing with – making dye is a lot like cooking. Bark likes to be cooked hot for a long time, whereas something light and leafy would be dealt with in a much gentler way. To turn the concoction from a colourful stew into a dye, you need to add a "mordant" like alum. It's a safe mineral salt that fixes the dye to fabric. It's gentle enough that, when you're finished, the dye bath can be used to water acid-soil-loving plants such as rhododendron or blueberry.

"I did it first as a science project at art school, where I screen-printed with mail order natural dyes," explains Katelyn. "I used madder, which is red. I painted vinegar on one print and baking soda on another – one turned plum purple and the other turned yellow. It was like magic. I haven't used synthetic dye since."

Katelyn quickly moved on from mail order. "I love the diversity of the experience when you pick the dye plants yourself. With powders you get the same result each time." Some people hate the inconsistency of natural dyeing, but Katelyn embraces the unknown. She also appreciates being able to handle her freshly dyed wet work without gloves. "It is so beautiful that you can touch them. With synthetic dyes you would never be able to do that."

> Many natural dyes are edible, which means you can use your pickings to both colour your cloth and make your meal

Red cabbage can dye a piece of silk an elegant blue, while red onion skin can produce a shocking green and yellow. It is indeed like magic

The woodland is a great source of both colour and inspiration, but the humble kitchen cupboard has much to offer too. Red cabbage can dye a piece of silk an elegant blue, while red onion skin can produce a shocking green and yellow. It is indeed like magic, and Katelyn is the wizard who can transform a vegetable box into a painter's palette.

As well as running Dinners To Dye For, Katelyn is part of a collective and shop on Balls Pond Road in Dalston called Here Today, Here Tomorrow. It was set up by four graduates of the London College of Fashion and is all about showing that there isn't just one way to be sustainable, but many. One of those many ways is to use natural dyes, and Katelyn also sells clothes in the shop.

We return to the warehouse, where Katelyn sets up her stove and gets some nettles bubbling. She makes mugs of hot tea and offers slices of sour dough with fresh nettle pesto and sweet dandelion jam. She talks about an upcoming event she's running at Hackney City Farm as part of the new Chelsea Fringe festival of gardening.

"It was the idea of people creating 'horticultural happenings' that drew me to the festival. I'm not a city person really. I think the fringe for me is about being a nature lover in the city. People here are interested in nature, but that love comes out in interesting ways because we don't take it for granted."

Railway meadow

Words by Lucy Scott. Photography by Rachel Warne

When Sue ran a tearoom in Suffolk, she liked to make the tables pretty for the customers. Every day, on her way to work, she would pick the flowers that grew wild in the fields near her parents' house, arrange bunches of them in jam jars, and place them on the tables – right between the salt and pepper pots and the menu stands.

When Sue moved to Homerton, her commute to and from her job as an accountant was quite different; at the station she passed through every day, there were no flowers. Just rampant brambles and empty drinks cans living in the verges, and graffiti on the walls.

But over the last four years, Sue has been doing the same for the commuters who drift through Homerton Station that she once did for the patrons of her teashop – only on a much larger scale. Today, Homerton Station is London's first wildflower station, with meadows of its own.

I meet Sue, founder of Friends of Homerton Station, at rush hour. She takes me through the barriers and up the steps to the platform, where homebound workers emerge from a train that has just arrived from the City. A man in a bright blue polo shirt, paper under his arm, walks up to Sue and thanks her on his way out. It's high summer, and what she has done here is hard to miss. The meadows that line the embankments on both sides of the station are lanky and luxurious; frail yet vibrant poppies, the rayed, purplish flowers of knapweed, and moon-faced ox-eye daisies bustle like the Londoners that pass by.

"A train station is the first impression of an area, and back then the station was intimidating. After a few years, it occurred to me that the way to change things was to get involved and do something positive," explains Sue, who has lived in Homerton for 12 years.

It was walking through Hackney's Clapton Park Estate that sparked her imagination. Once just an unremarkable urban housing estate, it is now known as the "Poppy Estate", after an initiative by the Grass Roof Company helped residents to create biodiverse community gardens for food and flowers there. "I thought, 'why not do this at the station?' So I started knocking on doors and getting volunteers together."

Sue didn't know anything about wildflowers, but she had an instinct that they would suit a station in Hackney. Shunning the idea of "suburban" rose bushes, she opted for a meadow instead; a more free-spirited planting that would be harmonious in its diversity – qualities that seemed more apt. "It comes into flower every year but it looks different each time," she says. "Wildflowers have a short flowering season so in terms of creating a public space with year-round interest, we couldn't make it harder for ourselves," she jokes. "But we put bulbs in so that early in spring there are snowdrops and bluebells, and we planted wild teasel, whose hooked spikes and conical flower heads look sculptural in the autumn."

Designing this bucolic landscape was a very urban affair, however, requiring negotiation with overhead power lines and engineering works. To help her and the volunteers navigate these challenges, Sue enlisted John Little of the Grass Roof Company - who still dedicates much time to the meadows to this day. They experimented with various planting techniques, including using fine ceramic chippings as soil (saving baths and sinks from landfill). "Infertile planting mediums work well for wildflowers because they don't need rich soil to survive. In more fertile soil, grasses and invasive species can colonise. But this way, the flowers have a chance," explains Sue.

Rather than just one lone garden, the meadows are the beginning of a chain of spaces that encompasses Hackney Tree Nursery, Middlesex Filter Beds and Mabley Green. And posters around the station direct people to them. "The posters show visitors something you wouldn't expect, and it gets people thinking about biodiversity and conservation," says Sue. Friends of Homerton has also created links with local businesses. To ensure that funding that Friends receives gets directed back into Hackney, a local printer handles the group's posters, local artists supply their artwork and meetings are held in cafés nearby.

Could this be a blueprint? "I hope so. I would like to do this along the route. The only reason I haven't is because there aren't enough hours in the day. But it would be great if Hackney became known for its wildflower stations," she says. We lean on the railings and look across at the flowers arching as a breeze blows across the railways. Sue points to a clutch of foxgloves, grown from seeds that flew in and took root unexpectedly. "In two or three years' time, this will evolve into something different. It is so hard to predict what that may be."

> Sue didn't know anything about wildflowers, but she had an instinct that they'd suit a station in Hackney

PHOTOGRAPHY: TOM HARTFORD

There may not be many traditional farms in the capital these days, but there are plenty of urban farmers. Farming for food, for community, and doing it in some fairly unlikely places.

This is Brixton's Edible Bus Stop, a productive plot created by local residents. Not so long ago it was a bland pavement, but today it's a focal point in which neighbours nurture plants and grow produce together.

There are no padlocked gates to protect the crops. Potato, gooseberry and herbs can be harvested by anyone waiting on Landor Street for the 322 bus. Gates are not needed for security either: the Edible Bus Stop has not suffered a single instance of vandalism.

Much of London's flourishing urban gardening scene is rooted in projects like this. At derelict sites across the city, green-fingered enthusiasts have been encouraged to pick up their spades and turn empty spaces into full-blown food co-operatives, growing all manner of edible plants.

Of all the diverse projects and their myriad purposes – community cohesion, education or profit – one feeling threads all of them together: a passion for nature.

These gardens are not simply growing spaces for fruit and vegetables, but labours of love for the people who set them up and who tend them.

It's 10am on Saturday, and the market stalls outside the church of St John the Baptist in Leytonstone are already a hive of activity. Before the volunteers have set out their boxes of produce, a frantic exchange has begun.

The market is run by food-growing co-operative Organic Lea in partnership with Transition Leytonstone. Every week they sell produce that they have grown on their nursery at the edge of the Lee Valley, and occasionally they hold popular seed-swapping days.

Today is one such day, and two women, each carrying vegetables in old carrier bags, are the first to do a deal. A packet of beetroot seeds is switched for a packet of sweet peppers, and a sachet of cosmos is thrown in for good measure.

A Spanish couple joins the crowd. The guy unloads his rucksack, and hands his girlfriend a stack of small brown envelopes, some of which contain tomato seeds from their native land. She places them on the table, and the crowd peers in. These are varieties of seed that the couple had trouble growing last summer in their tiny east London flat. But there's a man looking to fill his new allotment, and the seeds find a good home. He gives the couple chilli and lettuce seeds in return, and they head back to the bus stop, eager to get home and prepare their summer window boxes.

Parklands Walk and cycle trail

Alexandra Park

Highgate Wood

Queen's Wood

Highgate

Crouch End

Stroud Green

Finsbury Park

Runaway train

Words by Laurie Tuffrey

The gentle popping of tennis balls carries over the rooftops of Stroud Green as I make my way along the first stretch of the Parkland Walk. It's the day of the men's singles final at Wimbledon, but I've headed north to explore a new segment of the capital, leaving my flatmate by turns subdued or shouting at the television during a succession of bad sets.

Segment is probably the most appropriate word for the Parkland Walk: a 3.2-mile route that curves in a wonky, semi-circular arc from Finsbury Park up to Muswell Hill, skirting just below Crouch End and broken in two at Highgate.

It began life as a train line, and was opened in 1867 as a branch of the East Coast Main Line to serve north London's suburbs. In 1873, a further branch up to Alexandra Palace was added, and in the late 1930s a plan to extend the London underground proposed incorporating the track into the Northern Line.

A tube map from 1939 shows the walk as a dotted, "under construction" line, albeit one that would never come to fruition, the engineering work stalled by the onset of the Second World War and its completion afterwards halted by the establishment of the Green Belt. The line stopped carrying passengers in 1954, and continued as a maintenance line until 1970. The tracks were lifted a year later and the route was eventually redesignated as a park and nature reserve.

I join the path at the beginning of one of its two walkable sections on the masonry viaduct by Stapleton Hall Road, rising above the Victorian avenues of Finsbury Park. Once on the walkway it becomes clear that this is a natural footpath, even if it has been forged from railway cuttings, and one that is far better viewed at walking pace than being glimpsed through the window of a rushing commuter carriage.

The first stretch is dell-like, the ground swollen by a rich overgrowth of ivy laced with buddleia and the white trumpets of bindweed. Beneath the sound of the cheers being broadcast from Centre Court, one path branches off to the right and opens out on to a steeply raked patch of acid grassland that supports a fragile ecosystem of rare plants and insects, such as sheep's sorrel and the small copper butterfly. Alongside them lie a scattering of wildflowers and a wonderful stand of silver birches in the corner, gracing the meadow with their leaves' white haze.

I pass underneath the brick road bridge carrying Crouch End Hill and look up to see a sculpture of a spriggan, a Cornish green man fairy, peering out from one of its arches. Reputedly he, and this stretch of the walk, freaked Stephen King into writing his short story *Crouch End*. To a horror writer's eye, perhaps, this enclosed corridor of greenery speaks of the supernatural. Today, though, it couldn't be less intimidating as our spriggan leans out to bask in the sunlight.

All that remains of my next stop, Crouch End Hill Station, are the two concrete platforms, their expansive stretches now overburdened by cow parsley and nettles. Rather than being a sad spectre of past glory, the site looks comfortable in its inherited green vestment, inviting life. As I walk past, a group of people joke around while they assemble themselves for a photoshoot on one of the platforms.

However, it is the pathway immediately after the station where Parkland Walk becomes truly transportative, its repose lulling me into a sense of displacement from the rest of the capital. As the cutting opens out, the trees rise above: giant mature oaks and sycamores line the path and form a high-arching canopy overhead, a vaulting chlorophyll cathedral.

Further on, I cross over Stanhope Road. The road bridge, an unremarkable black brick and steel overpass, has been colonised by a spray of wildflowers: herb robert lines the bridge, while across it growths of bramble and field forget-me-not have taken root.

At the end of the 2.1-mile-long southern section, the walk breaks off at Highgate, separated into its two walkable sections by a still-in-use Northern Line depot. A pair of link-up footpaths take you through the ancient woodland of Queen's Wood and Highgate Wood, and on to the much shorter northern stretch through to Muswell Hill. Although this is less spectacular, it's worth pausing at the 17-arch St James Lane Viaduct. Here, a north-easterly vista opens up to your right, gazing on to a huge sweep of the capital, from Haringey down to Hackney, and with the City's hub of skyscrapers just visible to the south.

While London's Royal Parks are understandably renowned, this linear stretch of woodland perhaps surpasses them in its ability to seclude an entire section of the city under its canopy of leaves. It also retains the capacity to leave you feeling slightly adrift, albeit wonderfully so, along its naturally reclaimed trackbed.

Swift comes the swift

Words by Mark James Pearson. Illustration by Sue Gent

It's hard to imagine a more perfect example of a bird that is so urban, supremely exotic and perfectly symbolic of the arrival of spring in the city. It's also hard to imagine a London without them, being such a visible, vocal part of our street life, and with such a unique story to tell.

After an epic, punishing journey from as far as southern Africa, incorporating sea and desert crossings among other daily challenges, swifts finally return to London in late April and May. As harbingers of the coming season, there's nothing quite as life-affirming as their eventual arrival, wheeling and screaming playfully overhead, renewing bonds with their partners and bringing life to the greyest of spring evenings.

Superficially similar to swallows and martins, swifts are easily identified by a combination of characteristics, including their overall dark plumage, cigar-shaped bodies, short, forked tails and scythe-shaped wings, the latter feature earning them the appropriate colloquial name of "flying horseshoes". Their flight behaviour is also distinctive: as well as being extremely fast, they're often in acrobatic, swirling groups, with glides interspersed by a stiff-winged fluttering.

Their Latin name, *Apus apus*, translates as "without feet", which isn't quite as absurd as it may seem: swifts have proportionately tiny, claw-like feet, that are of little use on terra firma except as an aid in clinging to vertical surfaces. A strange, almost unique adaptation among birds, but more understandable – and not nearly as staggering – when taken in the context of their extraordinary aerial lifestyle.

Swifts feed on the wing (from within millimetres of the ground to thousands of metres up in the air), mate on the wing, and even sleep on the wing. Indeed, when a young swift leaves its natal home in a London suburb, it is unlikely to touch down again for another three years, clocking up millions of air miles over the course of its lifetime.

Their stay in London every summer is sadly brief, with most of "our" birds leaving by early August – equating to just a quarter of the year spent gracing the capital's airspace. Towards the end of their stay, swifts often become increasingly social, and parties of many hundreds may congregate where food is plentiful. The most impressive gatherings often occur over large water bodies, and London's ample selection of reservoirs provide the ideal place to enjoy the spectacle.

Look up into the blue for long enough on a summer afternoon, and the chances are, you'll see their rakish, acrobatic forms hawking insects above the blissfully unaware earth-bound crowds; check the skies just after dawn, and you'll likely find these early risers already cutting swathes across the morning light, or look out of your window after the sun has set and it's swifts silhouetted against the burnt orange of London's twilight.

> **Look out of your window after the sun has set and it's swifts silhouetted against the burnt orange of London's twilight**

As neighbours, they're about as good as it gets, being naturally gregarious, pairing for life, and even being good enough to hoover up countless thousands of flying insects on a daily basis. Thus, sharing tiny corners of our dwellings with them seems like a small concession to make. Swifts nest in the crevices and openings under the eaves of our houses and buildings, and are therefore one of the few species that don't just tolerate the urban environment, but actively seek and relish it; our streets are as welcoming to them as remote lochs are to Scottish ospreys.

However, their numbers are crashing alarmingly, and while there are various factors involved, swifts are suffering as a direct result of our collective negligence. London is evicting what is, arguably, its most iconic and magical bird, as a result of "improvements" to older houses, and a lack of available nest sites in new-build properties. With foresight and will from developers, local authorities, businesses and individuals, their demise need not be irreversible.

Swifts are the quintessential London bird; a bird that relies upon us and yet gives us so much pleasure in return, thrives where we thrive, and travels thousands of miles every spring on a journey fraught with danger, just to reach its home estate in Brixton, Barking or Bermondsey - arguably making for a more committed Londoner than any qualified cockney could dream of.

Stoke Newington reservoirs

PHOTOGRAPHY: MARK PEARSON

Although Stoke Newington's reservoirs are encircled by tower blocks and housing estates, they are also two of the closest substantial open freshwater habitats to central London. And although the pressures of ongoing development have had a significant impact on the area's biodiversity, these man-made water bodies provide a unique haven for birds and wildlife in an otherwise unforgiving urban environment.

This natural island within a wide ocean of concrete attracts a range of migrant species as they navigate across the capital in spring and autumn. Exotic rarities from far away, such as the red-footed falcon, Alpine swift and Siberian chiffchaff, have all been recorded in recent years.

During the winter months, gulls – among them the black-headed, common, herring and lesser black-backed – drop in to rest, feed and loaf about. In the hours before dusk, many thousands of birds can be seen using traditional flight lines towards wintering sites in the Lee Valley.

Checking for rarer visitors is worthwhile, and an Iceland gull bathing in the shadow of the high-rises is a perfect example of an urban birding epiphany. The appearance of raptors such as the marsh harrier, red kite and common buzzard in the skies overhead are increasingly regular during April, especially on warm, bright days.

A purpose-built observation platform in the East Reservoir's community garden affords unrivalled views of these seasonal comings and goings, and of the City skyline. Run by London Wildlife Trust, admission is free and the reserve is open most weekdays, though you are advised to call ahead as access is limited.

The trust also runs regular guided bird walks around the perimeter and hosts bat-detecting and moth-trapping sessions during the summer. The West Reservoir, to which access is also restricted, is a watersports centre offering sailing and kayaking for adults and children.

Both reservoirs can also be viewed in part from the New River footpath, a 28-mile route that follows the course of an aqueduct built in the 17th century to bring drinking water from Hertfordshire into north London. The path follows the north and eastern side of both reservoirs as it heads towards Islington. However, visibility from the footpath is limited, so it's worth paying the reservoirs a proper visit to engage with one of inner London's most spectacular wetland habitats.

Throughout the year

Spring at the reservoirs is marked by returning migrants and the activities of early breeding species. In March, there is a gradual changing of the guard: as well as resident species, common chiffchaffs and blackcaps begin to sing as early as the first week, and numbers build steadily as the month wears on. As the first willow warblers – many of them males in song – arrive at the end of the month, it's a sure sign that other long-distance migrants are only days away.

In the summer months, coots, great crested grebes, mute swans, little grebes and local speciality reed buntings use the wetlands as nesting habitats. Up to 15 pairs of reed warblers can be heard singing from the reedbed. August is the start of autumn at the reservoirs, as migration again begins to gather pace. Hirundines congregate after storms and showers, and large gatherings of swifts are a striking feature of late summer.

By September and October, autumn migration is at its peak. Thousands of woodpigeons pass over on their move south, as well as winter thrushes, finches, starlings and many other species.

Winter is quiet save for the impressive gull congregations, and common waterbirds include tufted ducks, gadwalls and shovelers as well as birds of prey like kestrels, sparrowhawks and peregrine falcons that circle the reservoir's perimeters on the hunt. However, extended cold snaps always bring surprises, from great northern divers to bitterns.

Getting there

The reservoirs are a 15-minute walk from Manor House tube station (on the Piccadilly Line), a 10-minute walk from Stamford Hill Station and a 20-minute walk from Stoke Newington Station. Many buses stop within a short walk of the reservoirs. The reservoirs also form part of the route for section 12 of the Capital Ring (Highgate to Stoke Newington).

Great crested grebe
A duck or coot-like bird that inhabits lakes and marshes. Performs an elaborate courtship display in which pairs raise their whole bodies upright, breast to breast.

Reed bunting
Predominantly a farmland and wetland bird. Typically found in wet vegetation but has recently spread into farmland and, in winter, into gardens.

Kestrel
Found in a variety of habitats, from moor and heath, to farmland and urban areas. The only places they do not favour are dense forests, vast treeless wetlands and mountains.

Life in a London cemetery

London's churchyards and cemeteries offer peaceful resting places for both the living and the dead, and are also refuges for rare breeds of wildlife that might struggle to survive and flourish elsewhere in the city.

There are 168 cemeteries in Greater London. This represents just 1% of the city's total land mass, but a cemetery in one of the inner boroughs will often form a significant part of its green space, and provide a crucial source of biodiversity in an otherwise highly built-up environment. More than half of the areas taken up by churchyards and cemeteries in London are classified as Sites of Importance for Nature Conservation. Churchyards and cemeteries are also a priority under the London Biodiversity Action Plan.

The success of cemeteries as wildlife sites has nothing to do with human remains, but stems from the fact that they offer a variety of habitats including grassland, scrub, woodland, and sometimes even wetland. The diversity of landscapes on which graveyards have evolved means that there is no typical ecology in a cemetery. This in turn makes them fantastic places to see lots of different creatures, and each will host its own unique mix – from those you might expect, such as bats and tawny owls, to those you might not, such as spotted flycatchers and song thrushes, and holly blue, speckled wood and orange-tip butterflies.

▼ Green woodpecker
The combination of mature trees and open grasslands in churchyards and cemeteries provide an ideal habitat for this bird.

St John's Wood Church Grounds, which was declared a Local Nature Reserve in 1997, is a fantastic place to see wren, blue tit, dunnock and woodpigeon. And Stoke Newington's Abney Park Cemetery, which is considered to be one of the most important natural sites in the capital, contains around 300 species of fungi, some of which are nationally rare.

Plants, unusual and otherwise, are able to make use of cemeteries' grassland habitats, and tombstones, monuments and the walls of burial grounds support a wide variety of ferns, invertebrates and lichen. Morden Cemetery once supported London's only colony of green-winged orchid. Kensal Green Cemetery, which was established on meadows and pasture in the 1830s, has provided a rich habitat for flora and rare species associated with ancient grassland, such as great burnet, pepper-saxifrage, sneezewort and common bistort.

This vegetation in turn provides food, shelter and an environment for nesting. Ivy, a signature plant of Victorian cemeteries, is an important source of food for over-wintering birds. A recent survey of Kensal Green Cemetery found that it contained 240 species of fauna associated with the plant.

◀ Hedgehog
The abundance of hiding holes and shelter are ideal for making nests or hibernating. The peace and lack of traffic also make cemeteries a favoured habitat for city hedgehogs.

▲ Holly blue butterfly

The caterpillars feed on the flower buds of holly and ivy. The butterflies, whose pale blue undersides feature small black spots, can be seen fluttering around ivy-bound hedgerows, trees and walls through the summer.

▼ Lichen

These extremely slow-growing plants, which are formed through fungi and algae growing together, provide habitats for insects such as marbled beauty moths, whose caterpillars feed on them.

▼ Wall ferns

A group of ferns associated with shady and permanently damp corners of churchyards or cemeteries.

Holy pilgrimage

Words by Laurie Tuffrey. Photography by Bertie Gregory

Wild is the word that comes to mind when you arrive at East Ham Nature Reserve.

As overused as the word has become, it feels right for this particular place, located in an east London churchyard. Although a crumbling redbrick church stands in the north-western corner, and graves dot and line the lawn, the vast majority of the space has been reclaimed by gloriously abundant nature.

The reserve - most of which is known as "The Wilderness" - is a beautifully ramshackle treat, but you'll have to commit yourself if you're going to visit. It lies at the end of a DLR line, the journey wending its way out from the City before passing Canary Wharf's nexus of steel and glass towers and the Thames's low-lying tidal marshes. Then, from Beckton Station, it's a 10-minute walk north under the motorway overpass, until you spot an overgrowth of foliage on the right.

London's Magnificent Seven cemeteries, the great necropolises built to relieve the overburdened inner-city graveyards of the Victorian era, have earned a legion of admirers, and it's not hard to see why: the stately West Norwood and the vampiric Highgate are both wonderfully idiosyncratic. East Ham's appeal, however, lies in its small scale, making it almost a microcosm of Highgate, though the east London cemetery pre-dates its northern counterpart.

You'd be forgiven for thinking that the nature reserve's thick tangle of plant and tree are the result of being left untouched, but far from it; a team from the Conservation Volunteers make a weekly visit. "It actually takes effort to keep the wild, overgrown look," explains Sandy Davies, a headteacher who looks after the reserve.

There has been a church on the site since 1130, and while the extant graves are mostly Victorian – with the oldest dating back to 1716 – burials have taken place there since the 12th century; so many, in fact, that East Ham is one of Britain's largest churchyards.

"When East Ham was growing as an industrial area in the 19th century the parish grew, and at one time reached as far as Forest Gate to the north and all the way down to the Thames," says Sandy. "The burials would have increased accordingly, and the churchyard stretched south towards Beckton, where the famous gasworks were sited."

As you follow that direction you can trace a barely perceptible path into a heavy weave of tangled ivy, cow parsley and sycamores, "The Wilderness", through which myriad routes twist. I follow one close to the road with only a foliage-covered fence separating me from the cars, though they seem much more distant.

A line of cedars runs down the path and generates a soft corridor through the forest floor, which is strewn in places with vodka bottles, food wrappers and other remnants of nocturnal visits.

Although there are no other humans, I'm not alone. A squirrel darts behind a tree as I make my way along the path, and I routinely brush away spider webs. Later, I see a tabby cat sitting on a tree stump, who, upon hearing me, descends into the knotted undergrowth with trepidation.

Having reached the reserve's southern boundary I turn round to try and orientate myself with the church – uncertain, with the graveyard's deceptive scale, of how far I've come. The church tower was farther away than I'd thought, lost over a fiery terrain of foxgloves.

> ## Its secluded nature means that passersby think the church is closed and the ground is unused

Carrying on, I pass by growths of forget-me-nots peeping out from the earth, and graves that lean and cant between the heady aroma of elder.

It is this tangible otherworldliness that Sandy finds so attractive: "This site is a real oasis in East Ham, and largely undiscovered by local people. Its secluded nature means that passersby think the church is closed and the ground is unused. But others choose it for their weddings because it has the feel of a country church."

We often focus on finding recesses in the city centre to which we can turn for moments of peace and repose. Sometimes, though, making the effort to extricate ourselves from the middle of the capital and going the distance to find an actual pocket of nature – rampant, sprawling and untamed – can provide its own rewards. East Ham Nature Reserve is one such place.

Make the journey, push through the overgrowth, sit back and feel time dissolve.

Dock leaves

Words by Lucy Scott. Photography by Tom Hartford

From the centre of a giant steel compass embedded in the woodland path, we turn clockwise around the world.

Swivelling south, north and south again, Steve and I read out loud the words inscribed on its radial lines.

"New Orleans, United States, 4,810 miles: dairy and grain," says Steve. "USSR, 1,203 miles: softwood timber," he continues, holding out his arm in the direction of an avenue of teenage oaks.

"Calcutta, India, via Suez, 7,965 miles: tea, cotton, spices," I say, turning to the grass verge behind me.

"When I was a kid you could blindfold me as I walked down the river, and I could tell you exactly where I was just from the smells," says Steve. "You'd get the cheese and butter around Tower Bridge, and the spices along the docks near Jamaica Road. And you'd know you were passing Surrey Docks, then known as Downtown, by the scent of the different timbers in the air."

Steve Cornish, Bermondsey born and bred, knows the lie of this land like the compass under our feet.

He remembers when the woodland was Russia Dock – one of the nine that colonised the Rotherhithe peninsula as destinations for ships carrying goods from Canada, the Nordic countries and the Soviet Union.

He remembers the time when the shifts ruled the dockers, and the dockers ruled the pubs; when the metal tracks, which still run under our feet, carried the cranes that transported timber to the barges; when the dockers left, the riverside warehouses were ironed flat and the men and women who made their living from words moved in; and, most vividly of all, he remembers the time when Rotherhithe was transformed from an island to which no outside soul dare venture, into a slice of prime London real estate.

Surrey Commercial Docks became the all new Surrey Quays as one industry passed on the baton to another. Between the early 1980s and 1990s, almost 6,000 new homes were developed in a land grab that has yet to cease.

South Dock became a marina for yachts, Greenland Dock became a watersports centre, and a supermarket sailed in to claim a berth in uncharted territory. But amid the commotion of money and deeds changing hands, there was one sliver of land that quietly snuck out the back door without a price tag.

And Steve has been fighting for it to stay that way ever since.

Russia Dock Woodland and Stave Hill Ecological Park comprise more than 16 hectares of wild space in the shadows of Canary Wharf, and have several Green Flag Awards to their name. But supporting this successful landscape is Steve and the Friends of Russia Dock Woodland, who are its fiercest guardians. They are up against daily battles for the wood's survival.

Steve takes me to the edge of the woodland to show me the hoardings wrapped round the land next door, which have been branded with pictures of soon-to-be-built executive homes surrounded by trees and landscape. Steve is chairman of the Downtown Defence Campaign, which has just ended a 10-year legal battle with Barratt over its plans for a scheme that has been marketed on the strength of its "woodland views". The developer initially wanted to build 15-storey blocks just metres away from ponds in which heron, kingfisher and reed warbler feed and nest – a development the group feared would have ultimately destroyed the habitat.

The campaign could not put a stop to the scheme, but its battle – funded at first with legal aid, and then by local residents all the way to the Royal Courts of Justice – won crucial concessions. "Through our persistence we've managed to argue the developer down to four storeys, and it now needs to leave a 12.5-metre buffer between the flats and the woodland, instead of the 3 metres it originally planned. But 200 trees have come down already while the site has been cleared, and 100 more will be lost." Although they lost their case, the campaigners' persistence has sent a warning to other

> When I was a kid you could blindfold me as I walked down the river, and I could tell you exactly where I was just from the smells. Cheese and butter around Tower Bridge, and the spices along the docks near Jamaica Road

developers in the area, who are now working with the group to avoid similar disputes before they submit plans to the council.

The woodland's status wasn't always so complicated. When Steve moved to Surrey Quays in the early 1980s, after Southwark Council built 300 homes in the area, he assumed that the promise of a new woodland for the new neighbourhood was too good to be true. However, the London Docklands Development Corporation (LDDC) – set up by the Thatcher government to regenerate the former docks of east London – made good on its commitment. In replenishing the land that once handled timber, the LDDC gave it a fresh purpose that seems somewhat apt: filling in the gaps between the mooring chains, tracks and wall capstone with grasses and saplings has led to a fusion of past and present that is still visible as you walk round today.

"All these trees you see here now were just tiny," says Steve. "The LDDC did an excellent job. It was well planned out. They built a healthcare centre at the edges, so that when people came out of the doctors they had somewhere pleasant to sit."

But almost as soon as the quango fulfilled its brief and left the area, the landscape changed. "I remember one Sunday in particular, this place was a mess," says Steve. It's an image I find hard to conjure up as we head back into the heart of the woodland, a laid back scene of walkers and dogs chasing sticks. "The trees were on fire, the kids had been using the grass we're walking on now as a motorbike track, and the local church had just had its stained-glass windows smashed with bricks. The vicar came up to me in the street and said 'Steve, what the fuck is going on?' That's when we said 'enough is enough', and we started to fight back."

Although the council funds two grounds staff to manage the site, it is the Friends of Russia Dock Woodland who are its spiritual keepers. By keeping an eye on everything from damaged signs to rubbish, the Friends relentlessly maintain the beauty of the space while fending off the planning applications that threaten its edgelands.

Amid these battles, they have scored many victories. Steve and I walk the pathways adorned with the hefty mooring chains of the woodland's history, and past a stream that was, not so long ago, littered with bike frames, trolleys and rubbish; today it is full of freshwater, toads, newts and fish.

Ahead of us is an empty ditch where a workman is busy finishing a project to extend the waterway with 80 metres of underground pipes; 150 volunteers from Ernst & Young are working on the scheme, which is being funded by Southwark Council. Keen to show Steve his progress, the workman pulls the cap off of a brown plastic pipe that juts from under the path into the ditch, and a crystalline streak of water bursts free. "When this is finished, it will be deep enough to call it a true wetlands habitat, as it was always intended to be back in the 1980s," says Steve.

A Yorkshire terrier bounds over to take a look, running ahead of its owners. Charlie and Lorraine, who've lived in Rotherhithe most of their lives, know Steve from way back and amble over, two other dogs in tow, for a catch-up. Steve tells me that Lorraine used to work at Russia Docks in the 1960s, and I ask her what has changed around here since then.

"I remember when nobody wanted to live here, when there was no Jubilee Line, and just one way on to the island and one way off it," she says, one hand on her hip, one on a straining lead.

"When the first houses were built it was like being in a dream: people who wanted to better themselves could afford to live here. But house prices tripled and people sold out to landlords who rented the homes out to a different person every year. So that sense of community disappeared. Now it's transient, like a hotel. But Russia Dock Woodland is an oasis, and it's all down to Steve."

I wonder if this transience is the biggest enemy in the battle to preserve the area's natural habitat. "We work with schools in the area so that the kids can feel a sense of ownership over the place," says Steve. "It is this that will really ensure the woodland's survival in the long term."

> Steve and I walk the pathways adorned with the hefty mooring chains of the woodland's history, and past a stream that was, not so long ago, littered with bike frames, trolleys and rubbish

Five footbridges that crisscross the woodland, and the hundreds of bird and bat boxes that are nailed to the trees, herald victories for the Friends.

Nature comes first, so that kids and everyone who uses the woodland are able to interact with it. "We are adamant that this place must never become a manicured park, with gates and rose bushes and swings. This is woodland, woodland, woodland."

Each bridge belongs to, and is named after, one of the five junior schools on the peninsula. Local blacksmith Kevin Boys has worked with the schoolchildren to decorate each crossing with sculpted arches based on the children's own ideas: bugs and insects provide the inspiration for St John's Bridge, flowers form the basis of the arch at Albion Bridge, and the design of Alfred Salter Bridge is based on trees.

"If the local kids feel part of it then that will have an effect, even if it takes 10 years," says Steve. "Now, kids come here before they go home and fish in the streams for sticklebacks. They have picnics, and they climb the trees. They make bird boxes, put them up and monitor the birds they see going in and out."

One night not so long ago Steve was out walking his dog in the woodland and spotted a couple of teenage boys, one of whom was swinging from a sculpture across one of the bridges. "I got ready to tell him to get down and say that I'd call his old man if he didn't. But before I got there I heard his mate say: 'Oi, get off. My sister helped build that.' He jumped down. And there, in one sentence, was everything that we're trying to do."

We take a trip over to Stave Hill Ecological Park at the north of the woodland, where some of the Ernst & Young volunteers have been working all morning with Rebecca Clark from the Trust for Urban Ecology, the organisation that manages the reserve. It's lunchtime, and as we arrive a team from the company's office has arrived with a camera to film a corporate video. A burly man in a chalk-striped suit interviews a few of the volunteers sitting on a bench about what they've been up to.

It's a typical scene over here, as big-brand firms from the City send out more of their desk-bound employees to spend time working in the voluntary sector. At Russia Dock Woodland they get stuck into projects such as the waterway extension, where they have been moving tonnes of chalk to line the new wetlands, or building fences.

"A big team like this can make such a difference," says Rebecca. "They have lots of energy because they are out of the office, and they get a lot done in a short space of time. It's like magic. But it is also great for the ordinary volunteers from the area to see these companies becoming involved."

Aside from the local kids, it seems the corporations whose headquarters loom over from across the river are also being educated about the value of this woodland space. To this end, the Trust for Urban Ecology is working on a research project to monitor how these volunteer days make people more willing to become involved in their local environment. "We want to know how attitudes and behaviour change over time as a result of getting involved in this kind of work," says Rebecca.

But for the men and women who spend their entire working day moving intangible things around the world, volunteering has immediate benefits too. "In one morning they might have built a dry-stone wall. There is nothing quite like standing back and being able to say: 'I made that'."

In the driving rain, Steve, Rebecca and I climb up Stave Hill, an artificial mound with a platform at the top from which Canary Wharf and the City can be seen across the water. At its centre is a relief map in bronze, showing the docks as they once were. On rainy days like these the water fills the docks and channels on the map, so that against the backdrop of the new you can see the area as it once was.

"There's nothing quite like this in other cities," says Rebecca, as the three of us take in the view. Such vastness of green living beside such vastness of grey. And, in between it all, so many battles for understanding.

> We are adamant that this place must never become a manicured park, with gates and rose bushes and swings. This is woodland, woodland, woodland.

The Double Tree living wall

The living wall that forms part of the Double Tree Hotel on Pepys Street – formerly the Mint Hotel – is one of the tallest living walls in Europe, and a stunning example of where landscape meets architecture.

Almost 200,000 plants provide the "bricks" in the wall, which extends across more than 1,000 square metres of the four-star hotel. The plants wrap around the building on all four of the elevations between the ninth and 11th floors. In the courtyard they extend from the second floor up to the top.

The courtyard wall can be viewed day or night through a glass roof in the hotel reception area. The higher levels can be seen from the surrounding streets, and even from across the river at Butlers Wharf – thereby achieving one of the designers' primary aims and bringing the sight of greenery to the upper levels of the City.

A wide range of species that will tolerate the differing conditions have been used on each aspect. Shade-tolerant plants such as Japanese spurge, elephant ear and ferns grow on the north side, while sun-loving sea thrift adorns the southern elevation.

Although the planting provides year-round seasonal interest to keep the wall looking beautiful at all times, it was also designed to provide habitats for a range of wildlife. The deep, dense layers of plants have enabled a range of microhabitats to take root, and provide a home for nesting birds. Bee hotels even provide rooms for the City's apian population.

At the top of the building there are two green roofs made up of sedum and wildflowers. Growing alongside the terraced area of decking and tables are planters containing rosemary and mint – which the bar staff occasionally call on when making mojitos. The roof also offers panoramic views of the capital's skyline, including the Shard and the Tower of London.

Through the year

During the spring, intense blue aubrieta flowers push up and over the mounds of tight green foliage on the east elevation. These provide vital nectar for bees before the insects turn to the neighbouring white flowers of the heuchera in late spring.

Come summer, tiny white flowers appear above the dense clusters of the white stonecrop on the west elevation, providing seasonal interest for butterflies and spectators alike.

As autumn approaches, the heuchera display orange hues, and there are splashes of purple from the flowers of the periwinkle. Tall spikes of violet-purple flowers from the lilyturf cover the east elevation.

During the winter months, the glossy, green foliage of Japanese spurge and ferns such as the scaly male takes over.

Up on the roof

Though not a new phenomenon, London's collection of green roofs is expanding ever farther. Although some date back to the 1930s, environmentalists have been campaigning in recent years to persuade planners, politicians and building owners to embrace them.

Happily, it's a mission that's proving successful. An audit by independent organisation Livingroofs, which promotes green roofs across the UK, found that 500,000 square metres – an area equivalent to Hyde Park and Kensington Gardens combined – had been planted between 2004 and 2008.

These creations bring welcome splashes of green to London's buildings, but they are also crucial in helping the city adjust to climate change, and it was this idea that encouraged the mayor of London to rule that major developments in the capital should incorporate living roofs and walls wherever possible.

Since green roofs ameliorate summer flooding, organisations such as Thames Water are taking them increasingly seriously, while their capacity to make buildings more efficient to run and obviate the need for air conditioning, makes them attractive to developers, too.

But just as important is the fact that living roofs are good for wildlife, and it was this potential for habitat creation that influenced experiments into green roof technology in the late 1990s – most notably the "rubble" roof at Deptford's Laban Dance Centre that was installed to provide a habitat for the black redstart.

Twenty years later, well-designed green roofs are now providing homes for spiders, beetles and other invertebrates across the capital whose populations have become increasingly diminished through the loss of their traditional brownfield habitats. Bees and nesting birds such as skylark, oystercatcher and lapwing are also taking refuge on living roofs.

Spotter's guide

Rosemary
An attractive and edible plant, rosemary is adaptable and is well-suited to roof gardens and window sills.

Aubrieta
Originally from southern Europe and Asia, aubrieta is a hardy plant that spreads slowly on rocky surfaces.

Scaly male fern
Common in the UK, the scaly male fern is ideally suited to moist woodland floors.

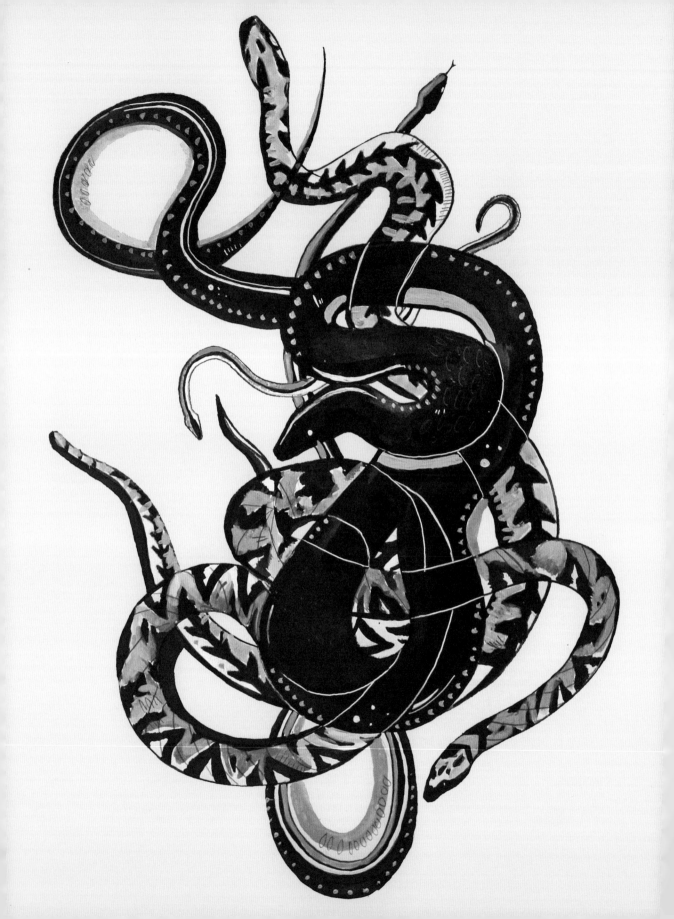

On the sly

Words by Richard Jones. Illustration by Daisy Hardman

Traditionally, serpents are viewed with less than sympathetic reverence. It's as if there is some deep-seated Jungian race-memory, back to the time when the first human stood upright on the African savannah and trod on a puff adder. Their secretive slitherings do little to endear them, but we should really be celebrating their beautiful sinuous forms, because they need all the help they can get.

The adder, *Vipera berus*, is Britain's only venomous snake, but it is too much maligned and overly feared. Sandy heaths and chalk downs are the natural home of this diminutive reptile – it rarely reaches more than 60cm – but it is known to wander far between hibernation sites and forage zones. In the north-east of the capital it lives around the edges of Epping Forest, right down into Woodford and Wanstead. It is reputed to frequent Woolwich Common, but nearby Oxleas Wood seems a more likely location. And, of course, it snakes its way up from Surrey's heaths into Esher, Oxshott and Cobham.

A quiet morning walk is the best time to find an adder sunning itself on top of a grass tussock or a patch of bare ground just off a pathway. Despite its bright crispness, the black zigzag pattern is deceptively cryptic; the slightly random coil of a basking adder's outline is completely broken up by the contrasting markings, especially if dead bracken forms part of the backdrop.

If you're really lucky, during late May or June you might just find a pair that are seemingly oblivious to passersby, their necks outstretched into the air, undulating wildly as if for some unseen charmer. These are males, vying in a show-of-strength competition for females hidden close by in the undergrowth.

Away from the drier heaths, the most likely reptile to be found – especially in gardens, and perhaps hibernating in the compost – is the grass snake. Much larger than the adder, the impressive adults can be as thick as your wrist and reach a metre and a half long. This is the snake of the pond or lake edge, the damp woodland ride or the marshy meadow hedgerow. A dull olive green, verging on grey, it is well camouflaged against the herbage, and immediately distinguished by its yellow collar and black neck marks. It is more widespread in London than the adder, and there have been a raft of recorded sightings down through Enfield, Edgware, Kingsbury and Perivale. In the east it has been sighted in Wanstead, East and West Ham, Rainham and Hornchurch. It is almost common through Mersham, Esher and Walton-on-Thames, and there has even been a sighting in South Norwood.

The grass snake is not really a constrictor, and more of a sneak-up-and-snatch predator. Frogs and toads are its staple quarries, but it will also catch fish, newts, unfortunate fallen nestling birds or small mammals such as mice and voles. Its scientific name, *Natrix natrix*, means "swimmer", and it is just as much at home in the water as it is on land. It swims like a miniature Loch Ness Monster, with its body beneath the surface and its inquisitive head held high. A splash and a ripple are sometimes all the clues you might find as it departs from its bankside rest to avoid you, leaving a characteristic S-shaped wake behind.

> A quiet morning walk is the best time to find an adder sunning itself on top of a grass tussock

But the "snake" you're most likely to find in London is probably the slow worm – not actually a snake at all, but a legless lizard. It is not particularly slow but, as one old identification guide neatly puts it, "it is rarely in a hurry". It seems more capable of getting around than any true snake, or perhaps it is just more tolerant of human disturbance. On the outskirts of London it occurs wherever there are rough, dry, grassy places, but it can also be found inside the urban heartlands of Willesden, Paddington, Penge, Streatham and Lewisham.

Shinier than any true snake, and with eyelids that regularly blink (snakes have none), this pale sleek creature is sometimes decorated with a chocolate-brown stripe down its back. It is often found in gardens, or derelict brownfield sites, allotments or railway embankments, and has a penchant for sheltering under rubbish – corrugated metal sheets, old tyres, carpet tiles, wooden planks and ply.

If disturbed from its hiding place it is also less likely than a true snake to take off at top speed and, after the initial serpent-alarm shock has worn off, you're more likely to be able to pick it up. The grip of its narrow cylindrical body on the fingers is firm and taut, and its tail-tip is especially prehensile. But be warned: the slow worm's scientific name, *Anguis fragilis*, is a comment on its brittle tail, which can be ejected in a trice before writhing on its own, disconcertingly, for several minutes. This is an excellent survival tactic: if the slow worm is in real danger, the attacker only gets the expendable tail tip and the "snake" escapes.

◀ *The cockney sparrow has suffered an alarming decline in London. But it can still be found making a home out of older buildings and ageing estates, where the cracks and crevices have been left unfixed.*

▼ *Originally a bird of sea cliffs, the peregrine falcon has adopted the city's skyscrapers as home. Here, he feeds on his staple prey, the feral pigeon – a descendant from his coastal neighbour the rock dove.*

THE

London Plane

Family tree

Words by Christopher Stocks. Illustration by Karolin Schnoor

Other cities have trees, but none has had a tree named after it. Elegant, grand and nobly proportioned, the London plane has two distinctive features that even the least arboriculturally sophisticated passerby can spot. Its bark, from youth to middle age, is smooth and mottled in large oval 'plates' of pale green, buff and buff-pink. Even more striking, as they dangle on long wires from their branch-tips, are what look like hundreds of blackened Christmas decorations – sooty little balls, often hanging in clusters of twos and threes. These are its mace-like seedheads, which appear each spring and start out as a pale green suffused with pink. As they ripen later in the year they turn a knobbly soft brown, before blackening as winter comes – each tiny angular nub being one among a thousand-odd closely packed seeds.

When you start looking you'll see they're everywhere. The London plane is generally reckoned to be the capital's commonest tree, and it's easy to take them for granted, but the city would look very different without them. They dominate the great streets and avenues, but especially London's justly famous squares, in which they are almost always the largest trees.

Yet this iconic symbol of London has two odd things about it. For a start, it is not to be found in the wild, and is actually a man-made hybrid of two different species of plane. Natural hybrids occur all the time, of course, but the species from which we think the London plane derives evolved on two different continents – Europe and America – which rules out a naturally occurring cross. The other odd thing is that we're not sure where it came from. It was first described in 1663, but for some reason early botanists believed that its origins lay in Spain, and it was often referred to by the Latin name of *Platanus hispanica*.

In fact it seems just as likely that the first London plane really did grow in London, in a particular spot whose outlines we can still trace today, even if the garden in which it grew has long since disappeared. The great plant collector John Tradescant and his son, also called John, had a famous botanic garden around the house they called The Ark, named after the extraordinary cabinet of curiosities they assembled there (through some slightly shady dealings

with one Elias Ashmole, their collection later formed the kernel of Oxford's Ashmolean Museum). In this garden, which was just off what's now South Lambeth Road in Vauxhall, they grew the first runner beans in England, as well as tradescantia and tulip trees. They planted planes as well, and it seems perfectly plausible that they grew both the American and European species in close enough proximity for them to hybridise. Though the site of their garden was built over in the 19th century, its boundary is still commemorated in Tradescant Road.

Whether the London plane came from Spain or south Lambeth, its incredible success has several explanations. Thanks to an odd quirk known as hybrid vigour, a hybrid is often stronger, faster-growing and more productive than the species from which it derives, and that's certainly the case with London planes. They thrive on the heavy London clay, and their flaking bark and leathery leaves render them virtually impervious to pollution. Ford Madox Ford may have thought that "London begins where tree trunks commence to be black", but even at its sootiest, plane trees must have offered the city a welcome splash of green.

> It's easy to take them for granted, but the city would look very different without them

There are wonderful examples to be seen all over London, though the best can be found in the old royal parks and the squares of Mayfair and Bloomsbury. Berkeley Square has some particularly vast and aristocratic planes, though sadly they're no longer haunted by nightingales. My personal favourites, however, are in Bloomsbury's Brunswick Square. There are many grand planes in this little park, some tall, some wide and spreading, but the ones I love stand by the path along its southern edge.

They have evidently suffered violence at some time, because although they're clearly ancient they're also less than 30 feet high. Fresh young foliage still sprouts luxuriantly from their stunted crowns, but their shape is extraordinary, with gnarled and venerable trunks that spread wide around the base but that taper upwards to a point, giving them a bizarrely conical silhouette. Are they the stumps of once-tall trees, their tops snapped off by storms or bombs, or were they pollarded at one time? Whatever the reason, they're among the most mysterious and beautiful trees in London, and long may they thrive.

Twilight transmission

Words by Lucy Scott. Photography by Tom Hartford

It's twilight at Ruislip Woods, and the bats have risen from their roosts. Skittering and sweeping, on the hunt, moving from one treetop to the next, they are unlikely to be aware of the eight strangers standing metres below them on the heath.

The night begins to take form and the familiar shapes of the daytime – branches, leaves and land – start to flatten. Sounds become richer, but more alien. And the eight strangers are tuning in, moving the dials on handheld machines back and forth, as if trying to find a distant radio station.

Taking our first steps, we leave the edge of our fading world and reach towards the edge of theirs. Tonight, we will walk these ancient woods with a new kind of map.

Ian fishes in the bottom of his rucksack for the last of the bat detectors and hands it to a tall man called Greg. Firing up his own detector for a demonstration, he explains the dials and how we work these in tandem to commune with the bats as they navigate the skies. The air fills with the transmission of crackles as we practise, though we pick up little.

Our faces barely visible now, we also communicate using sound, gathering around Ian, who explains how bats work. Echolocation, the system they use to get around at night, appears similar to the way in which our voices rebound on us when we shout into the mouth of a cave. Bats build up a picture of the distance from their prey by making calls and listening to the returning echoes. These calls are pitched at a frequency so high as to be inaudible to human ears.

Of the nine species of bat that are known to inhabit Greater London, this vast ancient semi-natural woodland at the end of the Metropolitan Line has six: pipistrelle, noctule, daubenton's, natterer's, the long-eared and the serotine. Each appears to have its own "station", using a specific frequency range that suits its habitat and the type of prey. "If you get a noctule, the frequency will be between 22Hz to 25Hz," says Ian. "If it's a pipistrelle it will come in between 40Hz to 45Hz. Move the dial until the clicking gets louder and that will give you a hint of what the bat could be."

Our revving of the dials finds nothing, but Ian reassures us: "We've never been out on a walk at night and not seen a bat."

> Tonight, we will walk these ancient woods with a new kind of map

Torches and headlamps are flicked on, and the search mission begins. Beams of artificial light make tunnels through the tenebrous territory, resting as circles on the fissured trunks of oaks and on thickets of the limp bracken that flop into our path. Ian leads us in close single file.

I think of Mad Bess, the wife of an 18th-century gamekeeper whose spirit locals believe roams the woods searching for poachers, and look through the gaps of trees at the last traces of light for comfort. Although night has already come to the woodland it has not yet saturated the area beyond the trees. As we walk, Ian explains that this fleeting space between day and night is the prime time for bat activity. Why they emerge during twilight is not fully understood, but it's believed to be the time when they are best able to hunt in safety. Right now, they have enough light to see – they are not, as is commonly believed, blind – but their predators will be at a disadvantage. Even the sharp eye of the Ruislip Woods kestrel is defeated at sunset.

Sandy, a lady in our group, erupts with excitement as her echolocator rasps loudly, signalling the presence of something just feet away. We stop abruptly on the path and begin swivelling dials in an envious bid to find it too. The noises from our detectors overlap, clicking and whirring in chaos. "Turn the knobs until you get the loudest signal," Ian reminds us. He catches up with Sandy, tuning his detector and scanning a chain of treetops that have all merged into one amid the blackness. "Hmm" he says. "By the type of noise and the speed it, I'd say it was a pipistrelle." We all join him in our search of the sky, driving our machines in the dark.

It's Ruislip's combination of woodland and wetland habitats that the bats find so compelling. The reserve comprises four wooded areas that make it the largest ancient woodland in England. Nestled among them is a vast lido, which provides an ideal source of midges and flies when darkness falls. The open heathland of Poor's Field, where we began our expedition, also provides a fertile hunting ground. It is one of the few sites in London where grazing cattle rather than mowers are used to keep the vegetation in check; as a result, it is scattered with small anthills and cow pats. "We've been doing it like this for the last 15 years, which creates fantastic habitats for insects and, in turn, great feeding spots for bats," explains Ian.

We take care as we traverse a damp plank a couple of metres over a stream. Ian, however, used to cycle these woods as a boy and is at ease in the dark, navigating the reserve as deftly as the bats above us. His familiarity is such that he can find his way through the trees without the aid of a torch. In addition to being the Ruislip Woods Trust's "bat man", Ian is a leading member of the trust's management advisory committee, which was set up to implement a 100-year ecological plan introduced in the 1980s. The plan's commitment to manage the site for wildlife is part of a tradition dating back to medieval times. Ruislip Woods itself has had just eight owners since the publication of the Domesday Book.

Ruislip's natural appeal means that the trust isn't required to do much to encourage bats to visit. It appears that allowing the land to work in accordance with its own natural rhythms is enough. "We do a little bit of management for the bats," explains Ian. "What we noticed 15 years ago was that some patches of woodland were completely devoid of them, and it was to do with the fact that there was not much deadwood around. Now, we leave almost half of the dead trees to rot because it attracts insects, and we have bats where we didn't previously."

One by one we shuffle into a small wooden observation hide next to a large lake – a part of the reserve that is usually blocked off to the general public. On the outer edges of the woodland paths it has become slightly brighter, and the last of the light bounces off the water's surface from the sky – a blue-tinged whiteness interrupted only by the inky circle of trees around the lake. Fixing our beams steady through the open shutters, we watch in silence as daubenton's bats skim the water for flies and midges just a few feet away, flitting back and forth through the beams.

"See them go," says Ian, in an excited whisper. Our echolocators, lined up along the open ledge, transmit clicks in rapid succession as if broadcasting machine-gun fire. "Those signals getting closer and closer together are the bats moving in on their prey." Daubenton's bats, he explains, have outsized feet with long fingers, which enable them to grab insects from the surface of the water; this, in turn, enables them to put away up to 3,500 insects every night. We all politely shuffle round the cabin so those at the back can get a good look at the water.

Although this twilight theatre is compelling, only those who are committed enough to do what Ian calls the "morning shift" will bear witness to the best of the bats' nocturnal behaviour. "It's then you'll see them come back and congregate before they fly to the roost. They do this wonderful dance and then swoop away together." Where

they roost can often be a mystery. However, Ian tells us the story of a night just recently when, after months of seeing a large colony of regular hunters move off from the woods and drop away behind the streets, he finally tracked them to the roof of a house at the edge of Park Wood. He counted 1,200 bats back through the eaves of its roof on their return.

Bats do not build their own roosts, which they use for hibernation and raising their young. Instead, they use existing structures such as hollow trees or roof spaces, and knowing the locations of roosts can be vital to ensuring their survival. Sometimes entire colonies will disappear from the woods because a house has had its roof repointed or the owner has undertaken repairs that block the bats' access points. "People often don't know that they have bats in their roof," says Ian. "They get work done on their house and then the bats can't get out or back in. About eight years ago we had a colony of noctules at Ruislip Woods, but they disappeared all of a sudden."

I ask him what is the best way of finding out if you have bats in your attic. "Bat poo on the window sills," he replies, laughing.

The damp air carries the scent of honeysuckle around the woodland, and our torches fan out and probe the world around the now wider paths. As our senses become acclimatised to the nocturnal habitat, some of us venture into the undergrowth alone, trying to catch the sounds of a passing pipistrelle. Ian takes the rest of us over to a bat box nailed to an aged oak. It can't be any bigger than a shoebox, but Ian reckons that there could be around 70 pipistrelles roosting inside. He holds out his thumb to give us an idea of their size.

Ian loves the altruism of bats, and the way they'll look after the young of another while it's out on the hunt. "They are higher mammals, just like dolphins or primates. They have one child a year and spend a lot of time bringing it up. That's a very different way of living to rabbits or rats, and why the sudden loss of a colony in a roof, for instance, hits them hard." Hearing this, it seems as though our worlds are not quite so distant. These are creatures that share something of our ecology.

We emerge from the trees and head to the beach. On the other side of the now motionless lake are the roads that brought us here. Familiar shapes of buildings re-form under street lamps that stain the sky with amber. The lights from pub windows across the lido plunge into the water's surface in thin shimmering lines, like signs pointing us on our way home. Our torch beams stretch back towards them, making contact.

Above, the bats curve gracefully, as the eight strangers return to their roosts.

> Senses adapting and gaining confidence, some venture into the undergrowth alone

Life on the water

An angler's year

Words by John Andrews. Illustration by Clementine Mitchell

For anglers everywhere, the year begins in truth at midnight on the 15th of June when, by the sodium light of a nearby street lamp and beneath the distant glow of the city, the new coarse fishing season opens.

Across the capital, lines are cast into the water for the first time since the middle of March, when the world was a different place: devoid of leaf growth, warmth, and the scent of a midsummer night, unmistakably rich and sweet; the cry of the fox replaced by the call of the owl; and the night air making everything feel closer and more resonant.

By dawn on the 16th of June, every angler in London is reborn, whether they wake by the side of water or within four walls. I am no different: since I first picked up a fishing rod almost 40 years ago, this day has been special, unlike any other. I can count the number of times I have been fortunate enough to fish on it on the fingers of one hand, and I can count the number of times I have caught fish on it on one thumb. There is a tangible sense that the world is new and everything is starting again. I have opened the season on the River Thames at Sunbury, on Highgate Ponds on Hampstead Heath and on a thousand imagined swims in between when I have been captive to a traffic jam, a delayed tube train or at a desk going nowhere. Just the glimpse of water is sometimes enough to sate or prompt the need to fish. Or the rumour that someone was seen walking across Hyde Park to open the season on the Serpentine, the mysterious lake where a 9lb perch was once found dead, yards from where Harriet Westbrook, wife of Shelley, drowned herself in despair in November of 1816.

June passes. July is often a windswept month of frequent westerlies, alternating between rain showers and shirtsleeves, when to get out once a week and fish for a few hours becomes imperative. The early-season feeling of mania and frenzy has passed and you can fish safe in the knowledge that with each cast you slow the clock to a standstill. There are vast shoals of bleak in the upper layers of every stretch of the Thames, and beneath them fat chub and lean dace lie up by the dozen in between the streamer weed, turning their bellies against the gravel with a silver flash. To take a punt at Wilsons of Sunbury and trot a float downstream on the edge of the weirpool is a delight. You think about the legions of anglers who have done so before you, the chime of the nearby church bells bringing you back from your reverie with each slow passing hour. This is summer, afloat, aloof, away with the angling fairies.

In August, the angler is first to note the coming change of season, the subtle shortening of the days, the mornings suddenly filled with mist and a distinct chill. Everything has stopped growing: the vivid green reeds, the lily pads in the margins, the leaves on the oak trees above your favourite swim. The schools are off and the city empties. For a brief spell the fishing stops too, for August is the dead time: the algae blooms are at their height, the fish are sluggish in oxygenless water and the occasional thunderstorm enlivens things, but then it is back to the doldrums.

And then comes September, the month when the thick weed begins to die back, the rivers fill again with the first rains of autumn, every species of fish comes on the feed, the banks crowd with anglers here for the harvest. In weirpools, backwaters and up against dam walls, the perch hunt, their dorsal fins proud, their stripes never more vivid. The vast shoals of silver fish threaten to break up as the upper layer of the water cools, but in sheltered pockets they gang up only to be surrounded by perch, pike and zander. Each week at the stall there are stories of new monsters. A 4lb perch from a secret stretch of the Thames, a rogue sea bass caught on coarse gear in South Dock, a double-figure barbel taken from a swim of a tributary that everyone said was finished.

October, and the telephone starts to ring again as the evenings shorten and the parlour room of the public house becomes the debating chamber of anglers all. A pint in The Southampton or The Pineapple, or The Lord Stanley or The Social is in lieu of the days anglers promise themselves come the autumn. After "pint?", there is only one word on their lips: PIKE. In a city of anonymous souls, the pike is guardian of them all, a gentle misunderstood hunter, more capable of being killed than of killing, found in the dark places where malevolence lingers: lock-cuts, dead-ends, flooded gravel pits, rejuvenated stretches of canal, in ponds half cleared by community schemes, in upturned recycling boxes buried in the mud, and in the dreams of anglers waking to the change of the clocks.

And so November dawns, to the smell of cordite from the fifth and the revival of coal fumes as fires are opened up in defiance of the smokeless zone. At the stall is a queue of roach-men, old-school London anglers, who have given their three score years and forsaken the ten for just one more chance of a two-pounder. Each passing year has given them another clue about where the best swims are and where the seed merchants who'll sell you the best hemp and tares ply their trade. They come, muffled up, full of wisdom and every now and again buoyed up by a glittering triumph, a fat roach from the Lea or the Thames or even the pond in the local park.

Christmas comes for the second time in the year, and just like the 16th of June it is a day when every angler wishes they were fishing but probably aren't. A cast for a chub before the bird is carved, a pike bung lying against the reeds like some lost tree decoration. If you feel a stillness in midwinter, just before dusk, then take note: this is how the angler feels in every waking moment, senses sharpened, expectant, alive and yet somehow so full of regret. Floats go under, fish swim away, leaves fall and the year turns into its final days before the angler heads into the leaden weeks of January and February, when in recent years the ground has frozen like iron and the water with it too. We are all suspended until the thaw and the chance of a final fling before the season draws to its close on the 14th of March. Then the angler retires, just as the rest of the world ushers in the spring, to three months of retreat and reflection.

> In weirpools, backwaters and up against dam walls, the perch hunt, their dorsal fins proud, their stripes never more vivid

Tidal treasure

Words by Lucy Scott. Photography by Jon Cardwell

The ice skates were the most curious of all the items on the shelf of lost and found. There were a pair of them and they looked new, Colgate white in the early evening sunlight and primly propped amid the clutter of discoloured things: mobile phones, a hairdryer and the worn face of a nine of spades. Pulled from the river, with the blade guards still on, they were now kept by the guardians of the creek in an outdoor trophy cabinet that all the explorers pass by on their way to the water's edge.

Someone in our group joked that maybe they had once belonged to an Olympic medal hopeful who had come to the creek to bury their disappointments. But with the ebb and flow of the tide, there is little that this city is able to hide here. The urban neighbourhood, with all its miseries, debris and wildflowers, is of little concern, and these waters have their own agenda.

This is Deptford Creek, and it was here long before the fishermen, shipbuilders and dockers forged industries in its landscape. A deep, mile-long ford gave its name to the place. It's a wild river, a tidal river, 7 metres high at times, and the meeting point for many characters. The silt-laden, salty waters of the North Sea and the Thames flow here twice a day. And then at low tide, the creek belongs to the clear, fresh waters of the River Ravensbourne – an 11-mile tributary that springs from a well just south of Bromley town centre.

It is at these times, when the water levels fall, that the riverbed provides the opportunity for adventure. And here we are, the night before the summer solstice, with waders on and long wooden poles to steady our footing, and about to explore the only creek in London that can be walked by man – the others being too short or muddy to contemplate.

Our guide, Nick, prepares us for our baptism as he leads us to the riverbed. His long beard and hair are flying high with the warm June breeze. "It's a wild river," he says. "It might be constrained by man-made walls, but the water is entirely wild. Things shift around you. And it is slippery. Go a foot down in the mud and you are stuck." We trample down the steep path, over the jagged stones, our poles striking the firm earth underneath. We head past grasses and then past angelica and hemlock water dropwort: botanical signals, we learn, that we are leaving dry land.

Nick is one of the guardians of the creek and a founding father of Creekside Discovery Centre, an educational resource run from a purpose-built wooden classroom near the water's edge that offers outdoor activities, field study and a year-round programme of walks to allow visitors to experience local wildlife, ecology and history. "The whole idea is to connect people with the river," says Nick, who has lived locally for more than 30 years. "There are lots and lots of people living here who are totally unaware that there is a creek running through it."

It is now 10 years since the centre was founded to protect and regenerate Deptford Creek after the surrounding area underwent significant change during the late 1990s (a process that continues today), largely as a result of the development of the Docklands Light Railway. At the time, the creek was considered to be no more than a final resting place for shopping trolleys and rubbish that had been flushed in after heavy rainfall. But ecological surveys were fruitful, revealing a diversity of aquatic and terrestrial communities living within the main channel, as well as in the foreshore, river walls and surrounding land; the botanical survey alone revealed 150 species of wildflower. Today, there are pairs of grey wagtails – "kings of the creek", as Nick calls them – nesting here, while kingfishers, herons, great crested grebes and cormorants are regular visitors to the water to hunt flounder, eel, sea bass and Chinese mitten crab.

The flow of the tide through the creek between the Thames and its tributaries – the Ravensbourne, Quaggy and Pool – is essential to the area's ecology. It is on the energy of these tides that shoals of flounder make

it into the creek from their birthplace in the North Sea. With every city-bound tide they manage to push a few miles on, resting in the mud when it turns. "The creek is an important nursery for flounder," says Nick. "When they arrive here, they are tiny and transparent. They spend the summers here feeding and growing. After they leave, we get huge numbers of goby who come here to feed before going back to the estuary in winter."

But the surveys revealed something else: that the shopping trolleys are an important feature of the riverscape. In the first clean-up by volunteers back in the late 1990s, 400 trolleys were removed in just one weekend; but when the Environment Agency compared the number of fish in the creek from before and after the trolleys had been removed, it found that the marine population had halved. "The creek is now only a quarter of the width that it was in Roman times," explains Nick. "So over the years it has lost natural features like reedbeds, which provided hiding places for fish and for small invertebrates looking to hide from the bigger fish that come looking for food at high tide. So maybe they're an eyesore, but we now control what we take away. The rubbish is important for a lot of the animals living here."

Legs swish through water as we make our way south and uphill along the riverbed, against the flow of the water. Two swifts make long arches through the clear sky overhead as they hunt in the dusk for insects. It's a picture of calm, but a week earlier heavy storms would have seen our group shoulder high with water. "There are times when the river is really dangerous, and it is roaring after rainfall," says Nick. "There's a saying that rain is good weather for ducks, but it's not necessarily the case. Last week our mallard was down to just one duckling and the geese were down to one gosling. The rest of the chicks were washed away."

All around us are signs of the recent torrents, and of water's capacity to change the landscape – even here, in this cityscape crisscrossed and edged with solid, immovable things such as train tracks, railings and bridges. On the walls, the vegetation droops down, as if it were still imagining the weight of the water upon it and bending to the ghost of its will. The mud along the banks is rippled with fissures, formed during high tidal currents.

"London is coastal," says Nick. "People forget that. We say that Brighton is London-on-Sea, but London is on the sea. That's why the Romans founded the city where it is, as the Thames allowed them to move ships up into the heart of England."

But water has the capacity for peace too. A fellow walker, Fergie, lives in an apartment overlooking the creek at Mumford Mills, a former Victorian flour mill. We pass by his window on our journey south on the river's path towards Lewisham. His partner, Nikki, loves to watch the water at night. "The best time to look at the river is in the summer months, at four in the morning," she tells me. "The colours are amazing. The water has a green glow to it because of the light reflecting off of the algae."

The algae keep time at the creek. At the height of summer they spread fast up the walls that run along the banks of the water, covering it like brilliant, emerald-green wallpaper. In autumn they turn the colour of burnt mustard. "You can tell the time of year here just by looking at the algae," says Steven, a long-time volunteer at the Creekside Centre. "They're seasonal. The colours around here are constantly shifting. In winter, after the algae have died, the waterscape is monochrome and bleak, but it has its own kind of beauty then."

We scour the riverbed, our eyes fixed on the search for treasure. Credit cards, an asylum seeker's ID card, plastic bottle openers and a child's plastic dinosaur are salvaged from the mud. Then we spot a limp, pale crab, floating free on the current. "Is it dead?" I ask, as it manages to evade being scooped up out of the water. We gather round Nick like primary school children, eager for knowledge and uninhibited by our collective ignorance. He lays the crab flat in his palm and holds it up for us all to see. We peer at it, inquisitive. "Is it dead?" he repeats to the group. We cannot agree. "It's an old skin, abandoned by its owner," he says.

"At this time of year crabs eat as much as they can and shed their skin as much as they can." He turns the shell over to show us its "escape hatch", through which it pulls itself free – legs, claws, eyes and all. "How long does a crab live?" someone asks. "Good question," says Nick. "I don't know for sure, but they probably reach breeding age when they are three or four years old."

After almost two hours we make our way back downhill to where we started. Nick hands around nets and shows us how to catch things. Mimicking him, we kick the mud for a few seconds, and wait to see what the water offers us. We are all eager to see what each of us has caught. Handfuls of shrimp come easily, but then someone lands a baby flounder and there is a commotion. It gets tipped quickly on to the tray of water wedged close by on the bank, so that we can survey it without drowning it in the air. Again, we all peer in, watching it stay close to the edges of the tray like a nervous ice skater at the edges of a rink. "That is so cool," says one member of the group. "How big do they get?" says another. "As big as your plate," says Nick. I wonder if there's much difference for him between the adult and children's classes. I suspect not.

"Say goodbye to the river," he says, as we emerge on to the land. We head back up the hill, and once again pass by the cabinet of rescued things – the symbol of all the stories we do not understand about the water, and never will. And then back we go to the world of adults, to a place where the game is all about pretending to know.

> The best time to look at the river is in the summer months, at four in the morning

Shine a light

Words by Helen Babbs. Photography by Jon Cardwell

Our starting point is Hackney Downs and our route is by way of water. We pass through a park plated with gold leaf and join the canal via a set of phantom gates, made by the lattice shadow of a wrought-iron gasholder. In the sun our route is warm; in the shade it bites. At Limehouse Basin we turn left and follow a blue lane east. The roads become wider and people less common. The smell is of fuel and salt.

The tributary Lea meets its master the Thames at Bow Creek, and this is where Trinity Buoy Wharf lies. The mud here is thick, glossed by water and patterned by river creatures. The landscape is brick, low level, sprawling and bleak. Beyond the curl of the Thames bad weather is moving in, a white fog of fine, fast-moving rain. We cycle through the wharf, in slow pursuit of a man on a penny farthing. He disappears, we lock up.

Hunger and weather decide our first move – to a marooned diner on the creek edge, to eat fried food and apple pie with cream from a can. Sitting in this metal shell with rain spotting on the glass reminds me of childhood holidays, when we'd be forced to lunch in the car while the great outdoors was temporarily lost to low cloud. Soft sandwiches behind steamed-up windows.

And then, at last, to the lighthouse. The "experimental lighthouse" in fact, and London's only one. It's not the candy stick you imagine. There's no red and white striped tower ringed with rocks and water. It's not circled by sea gulls and there's no wooden rowing boat listing at its feet. It's a squat Victorian brick warehouse with a metal and glass turret, surrounded by a wash of tarmac and parked cars.

Built in 1864, with the lantern installed two years later, this was where bulbs were tested and developed before being put to use out at sea. It was here that electromagnetic adventurer Michael Faraday carried out his experiments with light, including pioneering the use of electric lighting in the South Foreland Lighthouse in Kent. During the first half of the 20th century, the experimental lighthouse was where keepers came to learn their craft.

The wharf feels isolated and empty, but also busy with curiosities and the aura of eccentrics. There's the bright red lightship docked along one side, with an indulgent, rusty roll-top bath on deck. There's Faraday's precarious shed, with its pebble floor, secret drawers and stuffed black cat. There are mechanical sculptures, cogs and horns, all rusted into frozen poses. And there's a silent waterside moon clock that will tell you the time of the tides.

The wharf sits atop high sea walls that are licked with weed. It's low tide and a dark beach has surfaced. The clouds clear to the west and the view is of Canary Wharf and its cohorts: a thrusting mob that seems out of place and is happily shrunken by distance. A narrow metal ladder drops vertically down to the shore, with footprints set deeply in the sand at the bottom. They lead to a sputtering boat where someone unseen tinkers with the engine.

As we cycled into the wharf we saw the wreck of a lighter barge – half metal, half mud, and slowly melting into the river. Here, barges have been refashioned into a collection of pots and planted with dwarf apples. The trees are dotted among old shipping containers, which have been stacked on top of each other and turned into studios. They provide low-impact space to small businesses and artists, who inject this area with new life. There are pretty driftwood gardens, woven with nasturtiums, pepper plants and tomatoes, and a cosy sign warning you to beware the cat and the dog.

From 1803 to 1988, this was a place where navigation buoys, lightships and other equipment were made, stored and repaired. The wharf was populated by platers, riveters, blacksmiths, tinsmiths, carpenters, pattern makers and painters. Imagine the noise, the dust, the filth and the sparks. The blackened cheeks and the hardened hands. The dockside smog and smell. Do we mistakenly romanticise all this? Life became grim for the residents and fishermen of the polluted Bow Creek. And before 1803 this place was a riverside orchard. Today it is both relic and renewed.

Canalside

Words by Jojo Tulloh. Photography by Tom Hartford

What makes a perfect meal? If you ask the proprietor of the Towpath, a canal-side café in east London, she will probably say "simplicity". Those of you who are familiar with this small slice of culinary heaven won't require any further explanation. But for those of you who aren't, that one word will need some unpicking.

Why do I love the Towpath? It begins with its location. The café occupies four shallow bunkers at the bottom of a converted warehouse on a previously unlovely stretch of the Regent's Canal, one bridge west of Kingsland Road in Dalston. To get there you can arrive via Whitmore Road or, much better, walk or cycle down the canal. Where you start and how far along you go are up to you, but Angel Tube Station is a 20-minute walk away and Broadway Market is 15 minutes in the other direction.

On still days the canal is a deep, green vault of mirrored clouds: cormorants pierce the surface with serpentine grace, and plucky coots defend their patch. In May creamy elderflowers bloom, and you can forage for the wild rocket that sprouts out of the walls. Along your route narrowboats line the canal in endless variation. As you approach the café from the west you will see the community garden that has been funded and planted by the Towpath and its customers, and filled with climbing roses, sweet peas and bright green hops; from the east, brown awnings and mismatched chairs at metal tables signal your arrival. There are bike racks tucked away beside the bridge, and a flat terrace with blankets should you prefer to take your meal as a picnic.

Step up to the high counter made from reclaimed wood and you'll find an Italian sensibility at work. It's no surprise to learn that the proprietor, American-born food writer Lori de Mori, spent 20 years raising her children and writing books in the countryside just outside Florence. At the Towpath this approach informs the menu – a different one is chalked up each day, featuring only what is freshest and best in season – but it also extends to the service. Whether you have come for a coffee or a three-course meal, you are made to feel welcome and put at your ease. On top of all this, the Towpath's cook is the modest yet enormously talented Laura Jackson. Whether it is the homemade soft-scoop ice-cream, pasty made with crumbly pastry and served with rhubarb ketchup, or a leg of lamb slow-cooked for a party, you only have to eat here once to know that there is a very skilled hand in the kitchen.

And yet there was no real plan. The Towpath came about almost by accident when the newly converted units came up for sale. Lori had recently left Italy to begin her new life as a Londoner with her second husband, the food photographer Jason Lowe (they co-own the café). In the beginning the Towpath's "small is beautiful" approach was inspired by the winning simplicity of a hole-in-the-wall bar in Florence and Lori's realisation that people want less, but done better.

The Towpath's day begins with homemade yoghurt and granola, porridge or toast with homemade preserves. It is these early hours that Lori and her staff love the most, when all is still and light dances on the water, throwing

> ## Step up to the high counter made from reclaimed wood and you'll find an Italian sensibility at work

reflections onto the tiles. Around 1 o'clock the menu changes, and you might have a crisp salad of cabbage and brown shrimp or a delicate broth of chicken with wild garlic leaves.

One dish that's never off the menu is the toasted cheese sandwich made with spring onions and Montgomery cheddar, and served with an amber pool of spicy quince jelly. It is an oozing, tangy, sweet sensation and comes with a history: when Jason used to visit Lori in Italy he brought her Montgomery cheddar and her farmhouse garden had quinces, so they made jelly. It's comfort food of the highest order and went straight on to the menu when they opened the Towpath.

In the evening the setting sun gilds the scene. Salted almonds and olives appear and there are tiny rolls filled with truffle paste and cool glasses of pink wine. At night and at weekends they hold one-off events, such as wine tastings, Spanish food evenings and Catalan spring feasts; there are plans for a Persian dinner and a cinema night with food some time soon.

Whether you stumble upon it by accident or design, you cannot fail to be charmed. The Towpath is a true gem of hidden London; and while it may get busy at the weekend, it never feels like anything less than a labour of love.

Life in a south London river

◀ **Kingfisher**
These first appeared on the Wandle after the great storm of 1987, when they burrowed into the uprooted trees on its banks. They feed on aquatic insects such as dragonfly larvae and water beetles, as well as small fish and shrimps.

The River Wandle is 11 miles long and has two sources – at Waddon Ponds in Croydon and at Carshalton Ponds in Sutton – that meet around Wilderness Island, a statutory local nature reserve in Hackbridge. It's a river of many characters, running as a crystal-clear chalk stream in Carshalton before turning into a deep, brooding canal as it heads north towards the Thames.

The combination of flowing and still waters attracts a range of species, and the Wandle is a successful and thriving aquatic habitat, though this wasn't always the case. The river was declared an open sewer during the 1960s following centuries of industrial use, and a restoration project was initiated 20 years ago to restore the vibrant habitat that existed before the water mills moved on to its banks in the 19th century.

Better regulation, a fish stocking programme and huge local enthusiasm led the Environment Agency in 2010 to declare the Wandle one of the country's most

▼ **Three-spined stickleback**
These are common in the Wandle, especially in the slower runs. In spring, the male makes a barrel-shaped nest from dead vegetation and entices the female to enter and lay eggs. They can be found at Beddington Park, between Sutton and Croydon.

▼ **Freshwater shrimp**
The gravel lining of the channel bed attracts these pollution-tolerant creatures.

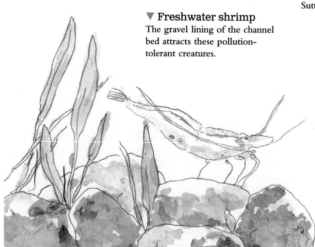

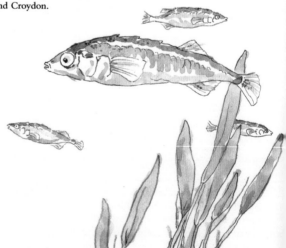

ILLUSTRATION: TOM BINGHAM

improved rivers. It is now home to eel, chub, grayling and dace, and has recently seen the return of its once famous brown trout. This makes it one of Britain's best urban coarse fisheries, and an attraction for walkers and cyclists as well as anglers. The 14-mile Wandle Trail, which follows the river from East Croydon to where it joins the Thames at Wandsworth, is one of the best ways to see it.

Theo Pike is chairman of the Wandle Trust, a charity dedicated to improving the river, and has been closely involved in its restoration. A keen angler, he was prompted to act after discovering its unique quality as a globally scarce chalk stream. "I was living in Hammersmith and looking for chalk streams close to London to fish in, and discovered this wonderful river with a historic reputation flowing through the badlands of the city," he says. "I met a couple of people who had similar ideas and we started doing regular clean-ups of the rubbish and pollution."

The trust has since developed an education programme that works with 9,000 children each year to teach them about the river's ecosystem, which now includes kingfishers and egrets. "By doing this, we hope not only the kids but also their parents will understand the value of the river on their doorstep, and that this will encourage them to look after it."

The river's anglers are also involved in its conservation. Theo is vice-president of the Wandle Piscators, an 80-strong fishing club open to anyone with an interest in angling and the river's biodiversity. The Piscators run fishing trips and a junior angling programme, and help to monitor the water by recording the number of freshwater shrimp and caddis. "It's natural for anglers to be involved because of their closeness to the river," he says.

For our story on the Wandle, see p62

◀ Watercress

The Wandle's constant temperature and its alkaline, mineral-rich spring waters make it the perfect habitat for this aquatic plant.

▼ Brown trout

If brown trout are to reproduce they need clean, silt-free gravel with a constant flow of cool, well-oxygenated water. All these qualities are to be found in the chalk stream, making it an ideal habitat. Small numbers of trout are returning to the Wandle, where they had lived for hundreds of years before it became polluted.

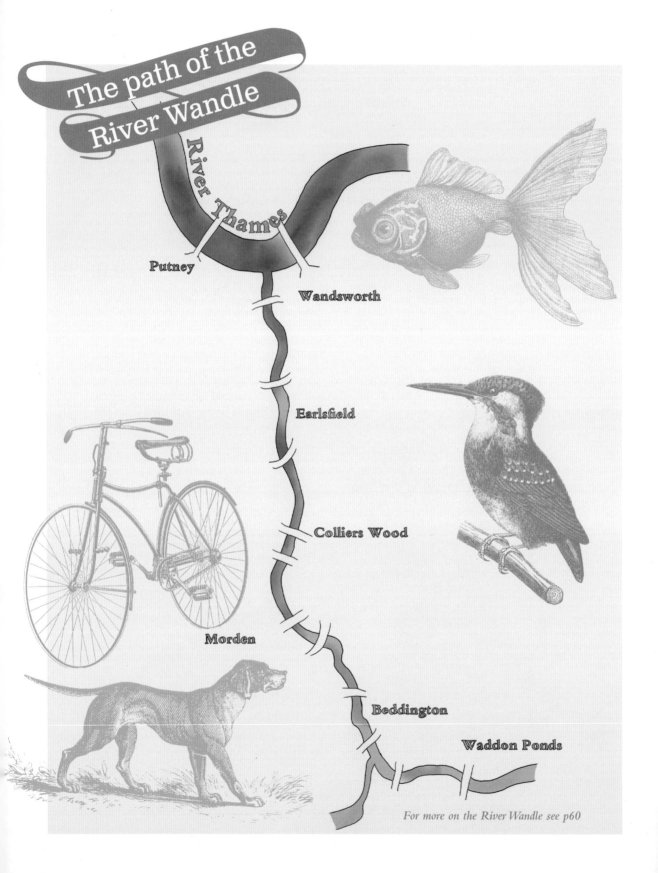

The path of the River Wandle

River Thames

Putney

Wandsworth

Earlsfield

Colliers Wood

Morden

Beddington

Waddon Ponds

For more on the River Wandle see p60

Chasing the Wandle

Words by Lucy Scott. Illustration by Tina Smith.

Past the fancy-dress shop, over the tram lines, past the pale terraced houses, through the subway and down the alleyway, we caught our first glimpse of the river. The Wandle, arrived alive. Once just a spring, and now richer. The liberal kingdom of Waddon Ponds. Coots lazed on it, willows wept into it, and on the horizon the towers of Croydon's old power station, branded in Ikea yellow and blue, reminded it of the industrial character it used to be.

It flowed on, escaped us. We lost trace of its tail as it darted ahead and made for its dark, concrete channel, where it could run discreet under the pavements, underneath carpeted living rooms where Saturday sport played out on flat screens. Under the kitchens where washing machines churned whites clean, to the gardens where brothers kicked footballs into miniature goals, and mothers knelt at borders attacking soil with trowels.

Blind, we chased it. Past the car park, metal works and removal companies of the trading estate, and a lady with a tartan trolley who sent us towards our own tunnel. Along a corridor of oaks, we caught sight of the water as it issued back into the light, visible like scattered ponds through the spaces between the nettles that lined the banks. Then the kingfisher, which shot from the undergrowth like an arrow; a brief electric-blue flash, and gone. Onwards, we rode with it, as the river skirted the ghost of a medieval mill. Bicycle wheels turning to its rhythm, keeping pace as the Wandle became wider, faster.

No more need for the map in my pocket.

You said you liked this bit the best. The park, on the other side of the terracotta bridge. An expanse. Beddington Park where the Wandle lay low to exhale. Where on warmer days than ours, it let children swing into it on ropes tied to the boughs of stately sycamores, and where it let dogs plough it into a million broken pieces. Where on that day, it paused just long enough for a bride and groom to pose with it, for a picture on a wall that wouldn't show the river take their wide smiles captive, and carry them somewhere else.

Wilderness Island. Where we heaved our bikes over the gates and searched the crazed vegetation for traces of it, making paths with no footprints. Nobody knew anything of the water; everything being so concerned with itself. The young horse chestnuts focused on their race for the light, the elderly ones wondering how long they had, and the orange-tip butterfly that apologetically hurried by, late for only it knew what.

By the time we reached the water's edge, whatever we'd been chasing had been and gone. The dragonflies, blue like the kingfisher, hovered over what had been shed: the translucent skin of the river spirit.

On the scent of its tail, on the scent of our instincts, we chased it, past playgrounds where parents talked, as children made the roundabouts go faster. Around the concrete edges of the park, and past the man whose dog we had not seen. Led, down the skinny track where the river waited. Watermeads Nature Reserve, where the Wandle looked at ease again. Where the anglers sat in the long grass with the pink geraniums, and next to the bait they kept in brightly coloured boxes. Where it flirted with the wild, and the wild flirted back.

By then, it was showing us all of its cards. At Ravensbury Park, where we stood on the bridge that strained across its generous body. Where we stared at the giant carp with the white-haired woman, who talked about her circus goldfish. As our words dropped into the water, the water gathered pace, on and on to where it once turned wheels for the mills, and where couples with walking sticks now sip cream teas facing the car park.

We were told not to expect much from now on. But as we headed further into the city, the water became ours. Wheels kept pace as it choked its way past the retail park and under the high street. On it pushed, exhausted, melancholy; not caring what it looked like now.

We were faster than it, speeded ahead while the warehouses on the banks held its arms so we could take a good look. It did not kick, but lay flatter, darker. Concealing its final truth.

We thought that was it. Where the pub that took its name from the river chalked up offers on blackboards, as it limbered up for its Saturday crowd. We assumed it was an epitaph, we assumed completion.

But sensing something, you pushed us on. From behind the rows of neatened terraces, we heard the sound; the gushing, the pushing, of the Wandle reborn. And there on the bridge, by the factory, was the water, stealing its way free. We leant our bikes against the railings and watched, as the Thames pulled the river towards it.

You said we had lost something. I felt it too.

There, where the waters met, we stood dumb. As the Wandle ran away with the Thames, and carrying all that it had been.

Here be dragons

Words by Richard Jones. Illustration by Amy Wicks

There is something primordial, antediluvian and slightly disconcerting about newts. Perhaps it's the crocodilian side-to-side swimming motion of the tail. Perhaps it's the miniature iguana-like pose as they hang motionless, their legs splayed, in the water. Or maybe it's just the lack of the plump comedic body possessed by their cousins, the frogs and toads. Whatever the source of the disquiet, newts' secretive and retiring nature makes them easy to overlook. Apart from brief references to "Sir Isaac Newton" in Beatrix Potter's *The Tale of Jeremy Fisher* and "eye of newt" as a dubious potion ingredient by one of the witches in Shakespeare's *Macbeth*, these remarkable creatures have featured little in the public's consciousness.

It may come as a surprise to learn that newts are relatively common and widespread in London, especially in the urban sprawl where garden ponds abound. The smooth or "common" newt, *Triturus vulgaris,* is the most likely resident and can easily reach new ponds by natural migration. My own very small pond in East Dulwich, raised above the lawn and held behind three layers of railway sleepers, was colonised by them, even though they had to climb up 50cm of rough old woodwork to reach it. The smooth penetrates further into the metropolitan centre than any other variety of newt, with Willesden, Battersea, Lewisham, Woolwich, Upminster, Walthamstow and Tottenham marking the inner ring of recorded sightings.

Like all newts, males and females are clearly distinguished during the breeding season, from late March to late May, when a wavy wrinkled crest along the back and tail, and a bright red or yellow belly speckled with black, mark the courtship plumage of the male. A good trick to find them is to examine a pond at night by torchlight; the beam will pick out the newts in the depths hidden by sunlit reflections during the day.

The palmate newt, *Triturus helveticus*, is the least likely to be seen in London, and is more at home in the acid pools of Surrey heathland or Epping Forest. Nevertheless, it has been spotted in Loughton, Swanley, Chiselhurst, Mortlake and Enfield. It is often confused with the smooth, though it is slightly smaller than its "common" cousin. The best identification pointers of the breeding male are his dark, webbed, hind feet and his tail, the crest of which stops, cut in

abruptly at the end, leaving a fine hair-like strand at the very tip.

The great crested newt, *Triturus cristatus*, is Britain's largest variety – and, at 18cm, a fully grown and fecund female is an impressive size. Although the adult breeding male is a couple of centimetres shorter, it is more dramatic, with its tall raggedy, fan-like body and tail crest, and its striking fiery underbelly. It is also slightly rough-skinned, earning it the alternative name of "warty" newt.

Nationally, the great crested is regarded as an endangered species, and enjoys official protection from disturbance or damage to its declining habitats. A loss of rural ponds and agricultural pollution of streams, lakes and ditches are often blamed for the declining numbers; but, unlike the smooth newt, the great crested has been less inclined to take up the increasing number of garden ponds on offer in urban areas. It is a lot fussier about its watery home, and needs larger, deeper aquatic habitats with plenty of vegetation. Nevertheless, it has been found around the perimeter of London in Leyton, Eltham, Bromley, Mitcham, Harrow and Uxbridge.

> **The smooth penetrates further into the centre than any other variety of newt**

After mating and egg-laying, all newts leave the water, and actually spend more time away from their home ponds than in them. From June through to February they remain terrestrial rather than aquatic creatures, living up to the name of the class of vertebrates to which they belong: amphibian, from the ancient Greek words *amphi*, meaning "both sides of", and *bios*, meaning "life". They lose their moist smooth skin and begin to look rather warty and wrinkled. Hiding under stones and logs, or deep in the leaf litter, they shun the sun and move to hunt insects and other small invertebrates by night. Newts can often be found in garden log piles, and the great crested is known to wander a good half-kilometre from its birth pond, keeping in the shade of woods, tree lines or hedgerows.

In the high, dry heat of summer, wandering newts may push deeper down into a moist sheltered spot and enter a hibernation-like torpor, reducing their metabolic activity to a tick-over to conserve water until autumn. They only return to the water, usually the original pond of their birth, in early spring to mate and lay their eggs. April marks the high point of this reverse migration, bringing them back to their watery beginnings.

London Wetland Centre (West)

PHOTOGRAPHY: SAM HOBSON

From inside a wooden shelter, a small party of observers peer through their binoculars, scanning the broad, watery vista in front of them. A few words penetrate through the hushed murmurs: pintail, bittern, teal.

You would be forgiven for thinking you were in the depths of the countryside, perhaps in the Norfolk Broads; but the row of towers in the distance tells a different story. This is the London Wetland Centre, run by the Wildfowl and Wetlands Trust, and nestles just south of the Thames in the shadow of Hammersmith's high-rise offices.

Building work began in 1995, when four disused reservoirs were shaped into lakes and planted up to create a variety of wetland habitats. Today, man-made sand banks are home to a sand martin colony, reedbeds shelter the elusive bittern, and a nationally important number of

shoveler swim in the lakes and ponds. The centre has also become an attractive stop-off for migratory birds, which come here to rest on their long journeys to Africa or northern Europe.

Since it opened in 2000, more than 200 species have been spotted at the centre. As well as providing a habitat for local wild birds, the centre is actively involved in the conservation of threatened species. Water voles, the UK's most endangered mammal *(see p84)*, were introduced here in 2001 and have thrived, their numbers swelling to around 350.

The main observatory and the six smaller hides enable visitors to get great views of birds they would otherwise struggle to see in the wild, and clear pictorial guides allow even the most novice of birders to identify the range of different species.

The ponds and gardens are linked by a series of flat and well-maintained paths and bridges, and the centre is divided into zones so there is plenty of variation to keep children interested. The Pond Zone is equipped with a remote-control "pond cam", and staff regularly run dipping sessions where you can borrow nets and see what you can find.

Walking through the World Wetlands area, you can take a close look at some striking international birds. Three o'clock each day is feeding time: beautiful wetland species such as the American wood duck gather round, and wardens are on hand to tell you more.

The waterside café also provides a tranquil spot for a cup of tea and a slice of cake after a hard day's birding.

Through the year

Sand martins arrive in the spring and nest in small holes in the banks. As their young hatch you can see them frantically darting above the surface of the water hunting for flies. The ponds fill with ducklings, and migratory birds such as the ring ouzel stop by en route to Scotland and Scandinavia.

As spring turns to summer, the wildflower meadows flourish, and the cackling sound of the male marsh frog resonates from the ponds as he calls to attract a mate. At dusk the bats emerge, and the centre holds regular bat-watching evenings in the summer months *(see p44 for more about London bat walks)*.

There is a change of cast as autumn and winter approach, and the swifts and martins are replaced by bitterns and overwintering ducks. The reduced foliage makes this a particularly good time for observing wildlife.

Getting there

Admission to the centre is £9.99 for adults and £5.55 for children. Annual membership costs £37, provides free entry to all Wildfowl and Wetlands Trust sites and helps to fund conservation projects. Reduced membership rates are available for couples and families.

The centre is a 10-minute ride on the 283 from Hammersmith bus station. Barnes railway station is a 15-minute walk and is served by trains from Waterloo and Clapham Junction. The site is also on the Sustrans cycle route 4.

Nearby natural wonders

About a mile west of the London Wetland Centre is the Leg O'Mutton nature reserve. Also a former reservoir, the reserve is a smaller, more basic site where you can watch wetland birds for free.

In the river to the north is the small, uninhabited, willow-filled island of Chiswick Eyot. At low tide it is accessible by foot from the north bank, but tides can change very quickly, leaving visitors marooned. Ensure that you've checked your tide timetables carefully before visiting.

Spotter's guide

Sand martin
The smaller cousin of the swallow, sand martins can be seen during the summer months flying acrobatically over ponds and streams, and perching on overhead wires.

Teal
A kind of small duck, teals are resident in Britain year round, but are particularly populous in the winter. The male of the species is easily identified by his bright green eye patches.

Bittern
Tricky to spot, bitterns sit still by the water's edge. Normally obscured by reeds, they move slowly and silently, looking for fish. *See p68 for more about the bittern.*

Bosom buddies

Words by Mark James Pearson. Photography by Bertie Gregory

Characterised by snaking necks, dagger-like bills and an elegant, stealthy gait, herons are a well-known family across the world. But while many Londoners know of their presence in the capital, few know that the city is one of the best places in the country to get close to not one but three species, being blessed with heron hotspots that are the envy of many more rural regions.

Grey heron, *Ardea cinerea*, is a common British bird, but despite their abundance, they remain an impressive, almost prehistoric vision - juxtaposed against the tamed backdrop of our urban surrounds, the sight of one lumbering lazily over rooftops, or frozen statuesque in a lake's shallow waters brings an affirming sense of timelessness to a contemporary landscape.

Grey herons are expert anglers, exercising an accuracy so fast as to be scarcely visible to the human eye. They're just as capable of taking amphibians, small mammals and even other birds if required; hence, the relentless mobbing of a heron by crows and gulls isn't quite as paranoid as it may seem.

In flight, grey herons are easily told by their size (dwarfing almost all other birds in London's airspace), their gangly legs trailing untidily behind them, and their long neck retracted into a tight S-shape when on the wing.

They frequent almost anywhere that holds promise of a meal, from reservoirs and rivers to small garden ponds, canals and even drier habitats. For breeding purposes, however, the capital's grey herons favour larger waterbodies with wooded islands, fashioning elaborate stick nests within the upper branches.

Having adapted well to life in the city, they can be found across London wherever suitable habitat exists, and it's no great challenge to find them. But for the real deal, a visit to a heronry during spring is a must. The most entertaining is the colony in Regent's Park. As a species they can be remarkably tolerant, but the birds here exhibit a tameness and approachability verging on the comical.

Go back only a couple of decades, and the arrival of a little egret, *Egretta garzetta*, within the city limits would have provoked hastily arranged sick days. As a supremely rare bird in the capital, it must have made for a breathtaking sight, illuminating the dark days of 1980s London. In recent times, however, it's become increasingly frequent, and they're now very much part of our avifauna.

Strikingly beautiful at any time of year, little egrets don an ostentatious breeding plumage that includes intricate, wispy crown plumes, highly prized among wealthy Victorian fashion victims. The subsequent slaughter provoked a group of women to form the Society for the Protection of Birds – an illustrious beginning for today's RSPB.

London records have increased in line with the species' wider range expansion, and while it remains an uncommon visitor to most wetlands, there are a handful of sites that are particularly favoured by them. Double-figure counts are not unusual at Rainham Marshes on the Thames, and Amwell Gravel Pits in the Lee Valley is good for views of this species at close quarters.

Little egrets have recently begun to breed in London. Not, as one might expect for an auspicious debutante, at an expansive nature reserve or lush wetland on the city fringes, but in the post-industrial landscape of Walthamstow Reservoirs in the heart of east London.

However, their choice of location isn't quite as unusual as it first appears. With resident grey herons as the perfect cover and protection, little egrets have set up camp within the heronry, blending in well. And as some local school kids proudly exclaimed after seeing their neighbours for the first time last year - where better for newcomers to thrive than among a raucous, bustling and diverse East End community?

The bittern, *Botaurus stellaris*, is the only one of the three species that doesn't breed in the capital, but it's nonetheless a local speciality; of the three, it's most likely to tempt non-Londoners inside the city limits, with very good reason.

Secretive by nature, bitterns require extensive, undisturbed reedbeds in which to breed, a rare habitat these days. Hence, there are precious few places where bitterns breed with any regularity, and conservation efforts are required to keep the expansive swathes of common reed in the right condition for them.

Come the autumn, a number of European birds head for our relatively mild, maritime climate; with the complexities of the breeding season safely navigated, smaller areas of suitable habitat suffice.

As such unpredictable birds, the fact that London is almost guaranteed to harbour bitterns every winter is extraordinary, and more than enough reason to get out of bed on a dark January morning.

The London Wetland Centre is one of the best places to see them, and the Bittern Watchpoint in the Lee Valley is highly recommended.

PHOTOGRAPHY: BEN QUINTON

The foreshore of the Thames lends itself to solitude, even in the central stretches around the South Bank. At first light, as the embankments and nearby streets become charged with the energy of commuters and traffic, all is quiet down on the river banks.

Every morning, Ian Lettice pulls on his walking boots and takes his easel and paintbox to the foreshore in Putney. There, with herons scouring the water for fish and barely another human soul for company, he captures the water's shifting colours, textures, light and shadows.

Although he has been portraying the riverscape around the Fulham Railway Bridge for years, he still finds a different picture to paint each day, as the character of the water and its muddy landscape alters with each new tide.

The Thames's urban surroundings hold no interest for him. Blocking out the rowers, sailing boats and barges that occasionally sail by, his attention is focused on the river's elemental wonders.

Working quickly, before one scene melts into a different one entirely, he sketches the way the warm morning light changes the colours of the bridge, or how the clouds' reflections look as they drift across the surface of the water and the pools on the foreshore. With just a few brush strokes, he catches the stories of a river that many never venture from the streets above to see.

PHOTOGRAPHY: RACHEL WARNE

London may have its fair share of outdoor pools, but for those wanting a unique experience for both body and mind there's nowhere quite like Hampstead Heath Swimming Ponds. They have encouraged generations of pleasure-seekers from far and wide to indulge in the art of wild swimming, and have inspired people to take up arms against the diktats of the health-and-safety age and strike a blow for individual freedom.

The three ponds are where octogenarians, with a passion often bordering on the religious, venture to keep that spring in their step; where the fearless brave the icy waters at Christmas; and where friends gather with hastily assembled picnics in tow on blistering hot summer days.

But as the truly committed who visit this wild woodland retreat every day will tell you, there's an art to swimming here.

It is not about a heads-down race for the finish, but a lazy breaststroke or a drift, belly-up to the sky, as you adopt a frog's-eye view of the world. Only then, among the ducks, trees and fresh air, will you find inner solace and relaxation.

And don't let the English climate deter you. When faced with the chilliest of waters – which can sometimes be found in the warmest of weathers – simply embrace the cold, dive straight in, and let the ponds invigorate your bones and spirit.

Life at sea

Words by Lucy Scott. Photography by Ben Quinton

It's 7am, and the beginning of a new shift at the lifeboat station. Aside from the navigation broadcast blaring from a black VHF radio on the table, the morning is starting gently for today's three-person crew. The tea urn is gathering steam in the kitchenette, it's lemon cake for breakfast, and the chit-chat is quiet as the guy who's just finished the night shift catches some sleep in the next room.

David pulls on his yellow dry suit over his black trousers and up to his waist, and sits listening to the Channel 16 weather report. To my ears, it's a complex, metaphysical poem about sea states, spray and the nature of waves, and a forecast for a place far away from here. But for those who work the boats of the Thames, it's the language of the world drifting right by these windows; and on this wet Friday morning, it is doing so at the rate of precisely 3 knots.

This is Tower Lifeboat Pier, one of four base camps for the Royal National Lifeboat Institution's search and rescue service across a 15-mile stretch of the river from Barking Creek to Battersea. The pier is positioned on the water, at the foot of the final arch of Waterloo Bridge before it joins Victoria Embankment. Yet despite its prominent spot underneath one of the city's busiest bridges, and the stark orange RNLI livery nailed across its roof, the charity recently discovered that fewer than a fifth of Londoners know it is here.

Keeping tally is a wooden board on the wall, like the ones in churches warning you which hymns are coming up: 234 for the number of launches this year, 123 for the times they've set out in darkness, 195 for the people they've helped, and 12 for the number of lives saved. In the 10 years since the service has been operating, its four London stations – here and at Chiswick, Teddington and Gravesend – have assisted 2,600 people between them.

The city flows one way, the river the other, and I sit by the window watching them both while David and Toni mill about preparing for the day ahead. In the top right-hand corner I can see commuters under umbrellas, drifting northwards across the tops of the arches to their desks in the Strand; a man in a brown cashmere coat appears, holding his oversized corporate brolly defensively to one side like a shield. But at eye level, the river shifts and swirls eastwards towards the sea, the waves moving the floor beneath us as it goes.

I mould my hands round my cup of tea for warmth, and the three of us watch the world outside the window as it gets lashed by the elements. The fleet of orange E-class lifeboats berthed next to the jetty rotate on the

water like hula hoopers. "The river's moving pretty fast," I say. "Today is relatively calm," Toni replies.

"Some days, the water and wind will really bash around the station," adds David. "On a really strong spring tide, if we'd had a lot of rain, it might get up to speeds of between 6 and 8 knots under Blackfriars Bridge. If someone is under there in the water, they'd be straight off downstream."

These rapid currents are the river's response to the pressures of what we have built. The city's ever-expanding girth, especially on the north side, has squeezed the banks of the Thames to two-thirds of the river's natural width, forcing it to be far deeper, faster and fiercer than it ought to be. David points to the rogue patterns in the water working against the current and whirling round the foot of a nearby arch. "Around these man-made structures you can get eddies, where the water will move counter to the current. If you were on a small boat out there, you'd end up going in the opposite direction to the tide."

The shuttling traffic on the embankment behind the station is one of the more dramatic examples of this foreshore development. If you stand at the grand iron gates of the Chelsea Physic Garden downriver, it is possible to judge just how wide the river once was. The botanical garden, founded in 1673, settled next to the Thames so that its apothecaries and plants could be transported back and forth by boat from its gates, and thereby avoid the roads, which were too dangerous to travel. An elaborately painted barge was once moored outside it, ready to take its botanists on "herborising" expeditions to collect specimens from around the city. Today, those gates are set back, and separated from the water's edge by a pavement, a road and another pavement.

Although there is a lulling atmosphere this morning, there's a sense that the mood could change quickly. If the bell goes, David and Toni will be up and out within seconds of a call-out, so at the sound of the phone ringing I jump slightly. As David takes a call from the coastguard, Toni and I chat about what draws her to the job. She is volunteer crew and, like all volunteers, spends two days a month working here alongside full-time staff such as David, a former firefighter. Most days Toni is a project manager at the Environment Agency, where she works on river restoration projects. But for many of the RNLI's besuited volunteers, their shifts are in stark contrast to the day job. "When I started working in London, I was doing a lot of marine conservation and spent a lot of time on the land and in boats visiting places," she says. "But as I progressed through the organisation to head office, I found myself spending more and more time at a desk. I joined here five years ago so I could still get out and see things."

Some of those things are not easy. Volunteer crew attend the same call-outs as full-time staff: the "jumpers" who seek to end their lives in the river; the children who fall in by accident off the bridges and walls; and the emboldened drunks who look for trouble in trying to swim the tide. Sometimes it's dark, and sometimes conditions are rough, as one 3am incident report from the day before my visit detailed: "Tower Lifeboat, Brawn Challenge, launched in torrential rain and poor visibility to reports of two men trapped on a pier near Greenwich … both casualties cold and wet, the injured man had fallen 10 metres on to the platform while exploring."
As David says: "The bell goes, you're out on the boat and life is as real as it gets."

"There are days after you've finished work that you don't want to really think about," says Toni. But she adds that the job's charm is in interacting with the many faces of the Thames: the September early-morning light on the water; the glassy stillness of daybreak before the boats wake and begin making their marks; and the coastal landscapes downstream at the Thames Barrier.
"The water takes on lots of moods," says David. "At 3am on a Saturday it can be a dark place, surrounded by lairy noises and sirens. And then first thing, as the sun is rising and the water is flat, it's a different world."

For Toni, it is in this compacted urban middle, where the heave of Westminster, Battersea and Vauxhall outline the river's flow, that is the most exciting. She sees it as an interchange for all the river creatures: the tourist boats that zip back and forth past postcard landmarks, the fish as they journey to nursery sites, and the migrating birds on their flight paths in and out of wintering sites in the Lee Valley. "Upstream, in places like Putney, you get living things – freshwater plants growing on the banks," she says. "Whereas here, everything is just passing through, both above and below the surface."

But it is also here that one can see how nature obscures the edges of what is manufactured and what is wild. There are peregrine falcons that use the Tate Modern as an urban "cliff" face, and herons that use the light from the street lamps on the South Bank to help them hunt after dark, later than they naturally would. Then further downstream, there are the shelducks – mostly coastal birds in Britain, which have managed to find homes in the banks around Greenland Pier where workers shuttle to and from Canary Wharf on Thames Clippers. "You see some bizarre sights," says Toni. "Wildlife has just adapted to the city. It does not see the environment as either urban or natural. A space is a space, and if they find one that works they'll use it."

The cleaner the Thames becomes, the further these boundaries around manufactured landscapes erode. The river was once biologically dead, but hundreds of restoration projects, tighter regulation of polluting industries and improvements in water quality have resulted in more than 125 species of fish appearing on the waterway, fostering a myriad of ecological relationships that have encouraged seals and other predators to the capital's shores. "You'll notice the sea bass up at Battersea and then, nearby, the cormorants ready to swoop on them," says David.

It's a success story that has been reflected in the architecture along the banks, and one that's clear to David and Toni from their unique perspective. The shifting attitudes to the Thames can be traced from the 1950s housing developments, with their backs to the river and fences to obscure the views, to today's luxury "riverside quarters", whose generous windows are turned out to face it.

"The river used to be so polluted that developers wanted to ignore it, and occupants used it as a kind of rubbish dump," says Toni. "But now, we see developers understanding the value of the water, and a lot of my work at the Environment Agency involves engaging with them, trying to get them to realise the value of it, and helping to prevent the city from expanding further on to the foreshore. We look at mangroves in tropical places and consider them to be wonderful natural resources. But the salt marshes of the Thames are our equivalent. The foreshore of the river is a great feeding site for birds and fish."

Outside the rain has eased down a gear, and we head to the jetty so Toni and David can do their daily checks on the two lifeboats. I ask Toni if she's optimistic about the river's future. "It's a balance. I see the river from an environmental perspective, but not everyone does and we are still trying to build into it. We've lost things we probably won't get back, like oysters from the riverbeds that helped filter and keep the water clean. But we've made progress too. Whatever the city wants to be we need to remember that the river is a fragile aquatic ecosystem and it's changing all the time."

As I leave them to the day ahead, wondering what it will bring for them, I look back into the river and spot a cormorant floating on the tide near the bridge, scanning the depths. Above, workers, joggers and buses still drift across. The city flows one way, the river flows the other. An awkward, unique harmony.

You'll notice the sea bass up at Battersea and then, nearby, the cormorants ready to swoop on them

Marko's vineyard

As spoken by Marko Bojcun. Photography by Rachel Warne

It's funny how much peace a row of vines and a few bottles of homemade red wine can bring.

I've always been a restless urban type. A country boy from Australia, I've lived in cities since the 1960s: first in Toronto and then in London. And, like many adoptive Londoners, I'd long held out the hope that one day I'd return to my homeland, or to a farm someplace else.

All that changed when my wife and I started our family, and our roots in the city were set. So 20 years ago I stopped dreaming and decided that if I couldn't retreat to the countryside I'd bring the countryside to me.

It began with an allotment in Muswell Hill and 15 newly planted vines. I like wine, but I also like projects that have only a marginal chance of success, and growing grapes in London was one that I believed fitted the bill. Twenty years on, I've learned that I was wrong on that front, and that it is possible to grow grapes in this city. But I have also learned through a long process of trial and error (and a large stack of books of viticulture) that it is important to get the right land, and to understand that mastering the art of making wine with some degree of predictability takes time.

I now have a 54 square metre allotment in the north-western corner of the Spring Hill Sports Ground in Hackney. It sits at sea level by the River Lea, and my vines take up half the plot. Many of them were transplanted from Muswell Hill: five madeleine angevines, one pinot noir and one kuibyshevsky, a Siberian and French hybrid. Most years, I manage to make around 50 bottles of red and white wine, which I give away to friends or, even better, share with them.

My allotment is perfect for vines because it sits under an open sky and by the water's edge. Vines need a lot of light, and here they can get a full day of it: from the moment the sun rises over the football fields opposite to the moment it falls behind the houses at the back. The vineyard's closeness to the River Lea means that conditions here are warmer because water holds warmth.

Wet weather can make it hard on vines, and lots of sun is needed to develop sugars in the fruit. But it's about choosing the right varieties to cope with the climate. My most productive variety is the madeleine angevine, a vine from the Loire valley that throws out generous bunches of white grapes each year and makes a muscat-flavoured dry white wine. It grows really well in London because

> My allotment is perfect for vines because it sits by the water's edge

even if the weather's grey during the flowering period, which it so often is in June, the vine will still set its fruit and pollinate. While my single pinot noir vine is precocious and erratic, and sends out its shoots in every direction, making it hard to prune and train round the trellis. It produces irregularly, is easily tired by one year of overcropping, and gives meagre fruit the next. I still don't know how to make a decent red wine out of it.

It is important to remember that it can take a long time to get your first harvest. It took me five years, a turning point that came after a neighbour on my Muswell Hill plot taught me how to prune. But when that time comes, it is so rewarding as you learn to work with the rhythms of the vines and the flavours in the grape skin.

As a wine producer you tend vines for so many years – some live for up to 150 – that you get to know them well. I used to buy grapes every autumn from the market, but I'd buy varieties I knew nothing about.

When you have your own grapes that you harvest year after year you understand so much more about them. Each season I record what happens, so that when the next year comes along I'll be able to look back and understand how I went wrong during the process of growing the grapes or making the wine – if I'd put too much sugar in, or left the skin fermenting for too long.

The main difference between my wine and a supermarket's is that mine is lighter in alcohol because the grapes are grown in less sunshine. It's only 11% at most, so it is the kind of wine you could drink at lunchtime.

The wine sold in shops also follows standard flavours in the international market: you get big, rich, semi-sweet red wines such as syrah, or zingy whites with tropical flavours. I'm not trying to imitate any flavour; I just want to get the best out of my grapes, and let them express themselves with their own unique flavours.

The taste of wine is determined by the earth and the season in which it is grown, and mine will taste different from the wine made from vines grown only a few metres away.

Next year's vintage will taste different from this year's, and it will be different again the next. My wine doesn't taste like anyone else's, and every time I open a bottle I have no idea what I am going to get.

Little Britain Lake (West)

Tucked between a busy road and the M25, Little Britain Lake is a truly unexpected urban oasis. Moments after driving off the lorry-laden A408 in Hillingdon, a humpback bridge transports you to another world. The industrial parks of west London dissolve into open fields, wildflower verges, cottages and grazing horses. At the end of this picturesque lane the view widens and you get your first glimpse of Little Britain.

Created as the result of gravel extraction in the 1930s, the lake has been managed to provide an excellent habitat for a wide range of waterbirds, butterflies and dragonflies. Throughout the year you can see large numbers of mute swans, mallard ducks, coots and cormorants. Man-made islands of hornbeam, willow and birch provide perfect nesting spots, and a large heronry rests in the trees. Early

spring is the perfect time to watch the enormous grey herons couple up and build nests, and to witness the impressive courtship dance of the great crested grebe.

Running alongside the lake are the River Colne and the Frays River, and the three bodies of water are home to a wide range of fish. Huge carp and bream can be seen basking in the lake, while the rivers support populations of pike, perch and roach. Hillingdon council regularly runs family fishing days, encouraging budding anglers young and old to come and have a go. Anglers are well served, with many designated platforms dotted along both the lake and the riverside. Anyone can fish in the lake; all that is needed is a rod licence. These are available online from the Environment Agency: environment-agency.gov.uk/rodlicence. Just remember that the lake is closed to anglers during the spawning period, which runs from the 15th March to the 15th June.

The surrounding paths are new and well built, making the area a particularly good spot for people in wheelchairs or with buggies. Some of the paths form part of the Colne Valley Trail, a 7-mile route running from Uxbridge to Rickmansworth. The trail takes in rivers, lakes and the Grand Union Canal and is suitable for walkers, cyclists and horse riders. Little Britain, positioned towards the south of the trail, serves as a welcome lunchtime stop, with its picnic table area and nearby pub, the Water's Edge.

Through the year

In spring the lake becomes a nursery to a large waterfowl population. As the ducklings and goslings emerge, the skies fill with swifts, swallows and house martins. Dragonflies and damselflies dart around in the reeds, and orange-tip, peacock and holly blue butterflies can be spotted on a warm day.

In winter the lake is a firm favourite with migratory ducks. Pochards, shovelers, gadwalls and even widgeons are regular visitors.

Kingfishers can be seen all year round, but you'll have to keep your wits about you if you want to spot them.

Getting there

It takes around 20 minutes to walk to Little Britain from West Drayton Station, which is served regularly from Paddington. The 222 bus from Hounslow or Uxbridge stops 300 metres away at the end of Packet Boat Lane. Access by car is from Packet Boat Lane or Old Mill Lane, and there is parking on site.

Nearby natural wonders

The lake forms part of the Colne Valley Regional Park, an area of countryside along the western edge of London that stretches out into Hertfordshire and Buckinghamshire. Colne Valley also includes Harmondsworth Moor Country Park and Iver Heath Fields, another good walking spot close to Pinewood Studios. A map of the park is available at colnevalleypark.org.uk.

Three miles to the north is Uxbridge Alderglade, a nature reserve run by the Wildlife Trust made up of a disused railway line and the surrounding marshland and woodland. The reserve is home to stoats and weasels, and to several species of bat.

On the water

The 23-mile length of the Grand Union Canal that runs through the Colne Valley is one of the country's longest stretches of man-made waterway without any locks. There are several narrowboat hire companies in the area, and the canal serves as a great jumping-off point for touring the Middlesex countryside or travelling up to Camden.

Pochard
Most likely to be seen in autumn and winter, the male pochard is easily distinguished by his bright, reddish-brown head, black breast and tail, and pale grey body.

Banded demoiselle
A type of damselfly, the male can be identified by the broad dark spots on his wings. After around two years as larvae living under water, adult banded demoiselles can be seen around slow-flowing rivers.

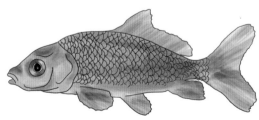

Common carp
Originally from Asia, the common carp can now be found across Europe. It is a freshwater fish, found in rivers, ponds and lakes.

Star sailor

Words by Tina Smith. Photography by Tom Hartford

The two enormous cranes looming over the water bring to mind scenes of Britain's industrial past. Years ago, they would have been stationed here to haul goods off of the cargo ships that sailed into these East End docks from places far and wide.

Today these cranes are themselves overshadowed by the colossal towers of Canary Wharf. And, where the old Victorian ships would have once moored, a prim row of sailing dinghies is being rigged and baled out in preparation for a journey through the twilight.

This is the Docklands Sailing and Watersports Centre, and I am buckling and zipping myself into a buoyancy aid ahead of my very first sailing lesson.

"We get all sorts here," says Phil, our instructor. "People see us from the windows of JP Morgan's offices and come down to see what we're up to. We also get locals from the Isle of Dogs, and people who've heard about us through word of mouth."

The centre – on Westferry Road, just a stone's throw from the Telegraph and Express Print Works - is a charity, and events such as this session help to subsidise classes for local children who might not otherwise be given the opportunity to sail. The session is a casual affair run every Wednesday during the summer, and for £25 you get two hours of sailing followed by a hearty barbecue and (as I later learn) a well-earned pint on the picturesque veranda.

Helming for us today is Emily. Tanned, smiling and unfazed by the ominous approaching clouds, she has the air of an accomplished sailor and immediately sets me at ease. She leads our photographer Tom and I past the brightly coloured bunting and on to our vessel, a Wayfarer sailing dinghy, which is apparently more stable than the others and ideally suited for beginners. "It's very unlikely that you'll fall in, but I can't guarantee it," she says casually to a visibly concerned Tom.

Emily learned to sail in her native north Wales, and instructs at the centre on top of her full-time office job. "I wanted a mentally stimulating career, but I'm mad on sport and love the water," she says. "This way I'm getting the best of both worlds."

"Sailing on the sea you have other factors to worry about, like the swell. But here the only factor is the wind. Learn to sail here and you'll get a real understanding of the physics behind it all," she adds, as we begin some practice circuits of the dock; a backwards L-shaped piece of water in the middle of the land that gives the Thames its characteristic deep bend.

I can see what Emily means. During our sail the conditions change rapidly. Although we're sometimes flying, with our sails full of wind, at other times we're making very little progress. Turning a corner as we make our way towards Crossharbour we are suddenly hit sideways by the wind, which has come tunnelling through the archway of an enormous dark building. We quickly change tack. "We call that the black tower of doom," Emily says, with a smile.

A loud whistle and the cry "three minutes!" signifies that the warm up is over and the races are about to begin. Slowly, and with varying degrees of ability, our flotilla shuffles back into a rough line between the markers. "Some people take the racing really seriously," Emily tells me. "It's all about tactics". She points at two dinghies that are perfectly poised by the starter boat. "They're there because that will give them the shortest route."

> During our sail the conditions change rapidly. Although we're sometimes flying, with our sails full of wind, at other times we're making very little progress

Emily relays the story about Ben Ainslie's tactical victory at the Olympics in Sydney. Having calculated that his chances depended on Brazil's Robert Scheidt coming in 21st or last place in the final race, he focused on keeping his competitor back rather than getting ahead himself. It paid off, bringing him the first of four gold medals. When I say to Emily that it seems a bit unsportsmanlike, she shrugs. "It's part of the sport," she says.

As we begin our first race the grey clouds that had been threatening us from the start set about their work. But through the rain I dutifully pull tack on Emily's orders, and duck as the boom swings left to right. In the confusion I have totally lost track of our route, and as we cross the finish line on our first lap I am amazed to learn that we are in second place. Tom and I exchange victorious looks, deluding ourselves that it must be because we are sailing naturals.

As we continue on our course past swanky riverside apartments, offices and towards Marsh Wall and back, narrowly avoiding collisions with other boats, Emily points out other instructors and regulars. Some first ventured down on their own and now sail with new friends. Some learned how to sail here as children and have moved through the ranks, while others are members of after-work sailing clubs who have come down from the neighbouring skyscrapers.

We keep an eye out for the local pair of swans and their cygnet, but they are sensibly keeping out of our haphazard path. Emily warns me that in previous sessions people have got a little too close and been met with busking wings and loud hisses from the protective male. "We have a Docklands seal too. She gets fed down at Billingsgate market and swims all around these docks. We've seen her sunbathing just over there," says Emily, pointing to the nearby pontoon.

Back in the changing rooms I find myself holding my socks under the hand dryer as I chat to a couple of girls from the Barclays sailing club, and we laugh through our dripping wet hair about near misses and victories stolen. The unmistakable aroma of barbecued meat draws us all upstairs and it's not long before we're chatting on the

veranda, our happy pink faces chomping hearty burgers and our crinkly fingers clutching pints of beer.

I find myself part of a gathering of instructors and regulars as they swap stories. "I learned to sail here when I was eight," says Sid, a young instructor in a hoodie. "I sailed around in that little square there, and I cried the whole time," he adds, nodding to the now flat water just over the veranda. "Little did I know I'd be standing here today."

Sid tells me he had ambitions to join the merchant navy and enrolled at the London nautical school in Lambeth, a non-fee-paying institution affiliated with the sailing club.

An injury put a stop to this dream, but he has continued to sail and has taught at the centre and overseas.

With his lifelong love of the water, he has applied to study marine biology at university. "I'll be three years behind the others, but with academic qualifications and my experiences here I should be in a good position to work anywhere in the world."

"Anywhere with a bit of water" I say with a smile. "Yeah, anywhere with a bit of water," he grins back.

Watersport hotspots

Highgate Ponds

Hollow Ponds
Boating Lake

Serpentine
Boating Lake

London Corinthian
Sailing Club

Chelsea
Kayak Club

Docklands Sailing
and Watersports Centre

South Bank
Sailing Club

Tails of the river bank

Words by Richard Jones. Illustration by Judy Lumley

Things have moved on apace since Kenneth Grahame's "Ratty" first appeared in *The Wind in the Willows* in 1908. The good news is a name change – the water rat (with its sometimes derogatory and negative connotations) is now almost universally called the water vole, a much more genteel appellation. The bad news is that *Arvicola amphibius* now luxuriates in the unfortunate title of Britain's fastest declining mammal.

Part of this can be attributed to changes in agriculture, and the dredging, realignment and canalisation of rivers for flood defence or land drainage. Since the 1980s a more insidious threat has emerged in the form of ferocious American mink, which escape from fur farms to make feral colonies along the same waterways that are home to water voles. Once widespread, and common enough for Grahame to place alongside those other wildlife familiars, mole, badger and toad, 95% of Britain's water voles have been lost in the last half-century – a tragic indictment of countryside decline.

Perhaps now, though, the tide for the water vole is turning. It is the subject of its own biodiversity action plan; it has become a conservation flagship species worthy of habitat restoration and reintroduction, and it has legal protection under wildlife law. London, generally free of mink, is proving to be a resilient stronghold for this charismatic little animal.

Not that the water vole is all that little: at up to 26cm long (plus 15cm of hairy tail), it is Britain's largest vole. Heavier built, with a blunter, chubbier face than the brown rats with which it sometimes shares its river banks, it also lacks any visible ears and is slightly reminiscent of an aquatic guinea pig. It swims well, but is not as obviously adapted to life in water as, say, streamlined otter or tail-propelled beaver.

Quite often its presence is only indicated by the loud "plop" of its squat body hitting the water. Dives, if they can be called such, beneath the surface last only about 20 seconds, and the water vole usually takes to water as an escape ploy, paddling frantically with its back legs – its nose, head and back just breaking the water.

Most water vole sightings are on the outskirts of London, where grazing meadows still have a grid of dykes and ditches. But they occur in Richmond, Dagenham, Dartford, Woodford and Wanstead, and there is evidence that water voles are spreading back into south-east London through Crayford and Bexley.

The water vole avoids fluctuating water levels, and needs soft earth banks to make its burrows: a maze of tunnels and grass-filled nest chambers. The entrances are sometimes surrounded by a "lawn" of grazed grass, cut short by razor-sharp teeth. Water voles are almost entirely vegetarian, eating leaves, stems, fruit, twigs and roots, but there are anecdotal stories of them eating frog legs (discarding the rest of the body) and grasshoppers.

Water voles are rather tolerant of some human interference. They seem unperturbed by dog-walking, angling or boating, as long as there is plenty of thick vegetation at the water's edge. They will also put up with lower water quality than many truly aquatic animals, tolerating heavy brown silt suspensions during times of floodwater, but not industrial pollution.

> London is proving to be a resilient stronghold for this charismatic little animal

Because they are legally protected (it is illegal to kill or disturb them, or damage their breeding places), water vole surveys are now a regular feature of any waterway management. One of the best ways to monitor the voles is not to try to trap or spot the animals themselves, but to find their latrines. Near the water's edge, on bare mud or trodden vegetation, look for small piles of the distinctive torpedo-shaped droppings, greenish-brown to black, 8-12mm long and 4-5mm in diameter. A well-attended latrine will have old droppings crushed and flattened, but topped with shiny new pellets. The latrines are the voles' way of marking stream-bank territories. Although not offensively dung-aromatic, they have a slightly musky scent if you can get your nose down close enough. About 130 metres of habitat can provide range for a male water vole, and perhaps 70 metres for a female.

Footprints can also be a give-away. The water vole's front feet have four toes, creating star-shaped marks in the mud; the back feet are five-toed, with first and fifth held out at right angles to the middle three.

London's water voles are, hopefully, on the ascendant. They have been successfully introduced to the London Wetland Centre, and future release sites on the Wandle have been identified. Meanwhile, habitat restoration and landscape conservation work is a high priority in Lee and Roding Valleys to help get "Ratty" back into the water. Soon, there will be water vole latrines everywhere.

Journeys through trees

Wooded wonderland

Words by Lucy Scott. Photography by Jon Cardwell

Friday's in the air. School is out, and shoals of kids flow towards me from every direction – from the doorways of newsagents and the top decks of buses, end-of-day sugary treats in hand, ties loosened. I am roaming a suburban high street in SE9, wearing walking boots heavy with mud and lugging a backpack, heading for Oxleas Wood – an ancient woodland less than 10 minutes' walk away.

It is a summit in many senses. It's the grand finale of a six-hour meandering walk, but it is also one of the highest points in London. From the top of nearby Shooters Hill, I am told, one can sit and gaze for miles south, a view that pulls the eye away, away, away – skimming the tops of trees and little else.

The wood is part of the first section of the Capital Ring, a 78-mile route around the city. I have been walking for hours. I am dehydrated, and I am lost for about the hundredth time today. But I imagine shambling my way through that old woodland at dusk, while the rooks socialise in the treetops, and find spirit.

I started hours ago at the Woolwich Foot Tunnel, in the sunshine and by the river – where families sat quietly, pushchairs parked, absorbed in the peace. There, the river is wide. The water is generous and so is the sky, reducing the industrial buildings on the other side to wafer-thin strips on the horizon. Like one of those pictures you might have drawn as a kid, where you'd take a crayon and colour a big thick sky in that bold unnatural blue, making all the best things disproportionately larger than everything else.

Hours later, having battled along the high street, I have made it out to Shooters Hill Road – a long, steep road that takes you to the woodland peak. So it is my feeling of fraud that is out of proportion now as I hail a bus, having cheated my way around the whole day. The Capital Ring route guides you seamlessly through London's commons, nature reserves and Sites of Special Scientific Interest. While I've seen plenty of London's natural world – birds drifting on the water seemingly for the hell of it at the Thames Barrier, wild daffodils in Abbey Woods, and the maze of woodland rides at Bostall Woods as I crisscrossed my route to here with that of the Green Chain walk – I have also wandered off-course.

The latest diversion was in nearby Plumstead, where I found myself lost outside a chip shop. A small group of locals gathered around me, then conferred as to whether there was even a woodland nearby, until I pointed to the trees peeping over the tops of the houses in the distance as proof. "Just take the number 90," piped up the bald man between sips of his Coke. "Walking it is gonna take you at least a half hour."

As the bus hauls itself up the hill, and the light starts to burn off into a white, early-evening haze, the entrance to what appears to be a farm comes into view, with a welcome sign advertising meadow hay for sale. Intrigued, I ding the bell and leap off.

I have stumbled across Woodlands Farm – perhaps one of the only working farms in London, and certainly one of the biggest. Its 36 hectares of land straddles the borders of Greenwich and Bexley and rolls with meadows, grazing fields, an orchard, hedgerows and woodland. We are just over a mile from the centre of Woolwich and there are pigs basking in the mud. There is a barn that houses (rather vocal) sheep and a small wooden table stocked with honey, jam and an honesty box. Over near the pigsty there's a man sitting on a white camping chair, with a peregrine falcon, which keeps gliding from his shoulder over the fields and back again.

It is hard to believe that anywhere in London can be quite so self-contained and aloof from the urban matrix. Many of the rural idylls you find in this city are ultimately defined by their context, the edges of them fringed by the built environment. But this is a rural landscape, and the eye tumbles from the grazing cattle in the fields to trees, to wildflowers and then to the woodlands behind, and the edges are hedgerows and stiles that only lead you to more.

It almost wasn't so.

There has been a farm on this land for around 200 years, built on the site of formerly ancient woodland called Bushy Lees Wood, which would have been as dense with trees as neighbouring Oxleas Wood. The farm has records and maps that suggest that the site was cleared in the 1790s for farming, villages and settlements. It survives today despite best efforts by some; first the Department of Transport, which, in the early 1980s wanted to run a motorway through the site, destroying two-thirds of the farm and Oxleas Wood;

> It is hard to believe that anywhere in London can be quite so self-contained and aloof from the urban matrix

and then from the Co-operative Wholesale Society and its plans for a carpet of housing here.

But the people rose up and the people won and, in 1997, the community group the Woodlands Farm Alliance, with the help of £600,000 from the Heritage Lottery Fund and Bridge House Estates Trust, bought the farm on a 999-year lease. From then on, it was agreed, the farm would be used for sustainability, conservation, education and the community. Its chief mission today is balancing the needs of this livestock farm with that of nature conservation.

Most of the work here is done by a band of 30 regular volunteers, and I meet one of their veterans shovelling muck in one of the outbuildings. Barry Gray, chairman of the trustees' board, was a protagonist in the farm's fight for survival in the 1990s. Now a recently retired hospital doctor, he works here most days. It's a busy time of year. It is early April and their flock of 45 ewes are being prepared for lambing. Barry tells me around 81 lambs (or "1.8 per ewe", to be precise) are expected over the next few weeks.

Behind him, a young guy swills water around a red bucket and chucks it onto the floor, sweeping as he goes. "This was knee high in muck a few days ago. The farm is not mechanised so everything is done by hand," he says. "The work here is very labour-intensive. There's a tractor in the yard that's circa 1970, but that's about it. If muck needs moving, we do it ourselves, there's no scraper to do it or digger to move it. It's hard but you get a sense of achievement."

Woodlands is not a petting farm; the animals here are its bread and butter. The pigs are slaughtered for pork. Eggs are sold from the chickens and ducks, honey from the beehives, and damsons are harvested from the nearby woodlands to make jam. The meadows are cut for hay, and logs are sold for firewood – both of which provide much of the farm's livelihood. There is no luxury of sentimentality here.

"We are a proper farm, in the sense that what we make and grow here goes back in," explains its education officer, Hannah Forshaw, who runs weekly classes for local schools. We lean on the gate, watching their two pigs, George and Ginger, as they laze in the mud. The peregrine swoops overhead. "We had hoped Ginger would get pregnant but she hasn't managed it, maybe because she's too old. Pigs are expensive, so if they don't produce piglets, we can't sell the meat and that means they aren't economically viable." "So, you're sending her to the a-b-a-t-t-o-i-r?" I whisper. "I'm afraid so," she whispers back.

> Woodlands is not a petting farm; the animals here are its bread and butter

But there are more charmed creatures here. Woodlands has been designated a High Level Stewardship site by Natural England, which aims to create a habitat of mosaics for specific Biodiversity Action Plan species and protect soils and watercourses. Woodlands is the only farm in London in the scheme. "The idea is that vegetation develops naturally for a set period of time, and it allows us to use the land for farming but ensures we conserve the land so the site works holistically," says Hannah. In practice, this means limited grazing of animals to allow wildflowers in the meadows chance to grow, and fertiliser is not used either.

There are more than two miles of hedgerows across the farm, and new ones are being planted – Woodlands' contribution to rectifying the untold damage brought to bear on many plant and animal species, as almost half of Britain's hedgerows have vanished since the Second World War. "The wildlife is responding to what we have done and birds are nesting in them," says Barry. While they finish mucking out, Hannah and Barry send me off to wander alone through their young orchard, which is formed of row upon row of fruit and nut trees. Money was raised to plant and nurture the site for the benefit of wildlife, rather than as a commercial venture, and local varieties and those of historical importance have been planted: Medlar trees, Concorde pears, Kentish Red Cherry trees, Kentish plums, as well as London apple varieties such as Cellini, Fearn's Pippin, Merton Charm, Merton Russet, Storey's Seedling and London's Pippin.

Although most of the produce will be left for wildlife, the orchard is used as an educational resource for classes on pruning and grafting. The trees are still skinny but the field is a shower of spring blossom, and the volunteers are excited about its future, when the trees will be so tall that ladders will be needed to climb them.

Thoughts of climbing remind me I still have my own summit to conquer, before a sky now blushed with peach collapses into darkness. I set off towards the thicket of trees over the road, as the rooks chatter, and make my way up Shooters Hill.

At its peak I sit, with the land sloping away from me, trying to fathom what bits of city lay underneath the canopy of trees. Across the green, families, pushchairs parked, are absorbed in the peace. It was just as the day had begun.

Nature, wide and generous, with all that is good out of proportion.

Woodlands Farm
Trust

We are a charity -
...donations welcome

Woodlands Far

Shooters Hill Road.

Animals.

Bantam hens/hens
Cows.
Ducks.
Guinea pigs.
Pigs

A healthy harvest

Words by Lucy Scott. Photography by Jon Cardwell

In the grounds of Bethlem Royal Hospital is an orchard, an orchard that harbours stories old and new.

It's a breezy day, and a strong wind is blowing sunshine across the rows of trees. The sight of this early spring breeze freeing the leaves is a tale in itself. Not so very long ago, these trees were incarcerated under a thicket of brambles. It was so thick and so tall that light and wind could barely penetrate, obscuring what lay beneath. If it hadn't been for the few determined boughs of the old Bramley apple trees that were strong enough to force their escape, then this family of trees, now one of London's largest orchards, would have faded from collective memory.

Peter O' Hare, head of occupational therapy at the hospital, was struck by the sight of these branches as they thrust through the thicket, apples and all, in a plea to alert passersby to the treasures hidden within. So over the last few years, he has been working with the London Orchard Project and patients at the hospital to return the orchard to its former glory – for the benefit not only of the city's cultural heritage, but of the patients themselves.

Together, we weave through row after row, each different from the last. There's Pitmaston Pineapple, Worcester Pearmain and Grenadier, and a couple of varieties of plum. There is a row of old, hefty Monarch trees, which gives sculpture to the orchard while the saplings planted in the place of trees that did not survive take root. Peter is closely eyeing the wounds of this new generation for signs that this spring's "grafting" work has been successful. Fruit trees do not come true from seeds or pips but by joining new branches onto the stems – or rootstock – of old trees. So to bring new varieties into the orchard, stems have been "rind grafted" onto the branches of existing trees. Peter fiddles with the tape around the graft, checking there are no signs of rot. He seems hopeful.

The orchard's story is entangled with the history of mental health care, and our changing attitudes to nature and its power to heal.

Bethlem's home here in Bromley is its fourth. It is an extensive site, defined by trees and meadows with the hospital divided into small blocks dotted throughout the site. Pathways meander through birch, horse chestnut and wild cherry. In spring, daffodils, crocus and bluebells carpet the extensive lawns. In summer, its large wildflower meadow sways with red clover, buttercups and knapweed.

It was the rural setting of a former farm and stately home that appealed when the hospital was searching for new premises in 1930. By then, the monolithic buildings of its former homes at Moorfields and St George's Fields had fallen from favour, so this south London idyll was deemed the perfect place to provide light, air, space and gardens for patients and staff alike.

The philosophy was a world away from its first incarnation as the Bethlem asylum at Bishopsgate – infamous for its barbaric treatment of the mentally ill. As treatment progressed, from the 1850s onwards, the notion of environmental therapy had begun to gain a foothold in the concept of recovery, with the use of restraint being abandoned entirely at Bethlem, and flowers and aviaries introduced on wards. But by the time the hospital made it to Bromley in 1930, the natural world was to take central stage. Each ward had its own building, dining room and garden that were arranged like villas over 100 hectares of grounds.

"A lot of the landscape from the old stately home was kept as it was, including the walled kitchen garden. Patients became involved in the farm work and gardening, and were encouraged to engage with the natural environment," explains Peter.

For some years that followed, the garden and orchard provided the hospital with fresh vegetables and fruit, even grapefruit grown in tropical Victorian glasshouses. But then things changed. When Peter joined the hospital 20 years ago, the idea of the environment as key to mental health treatment had become a thorny issue. Textbooks were altered, patients were taken indoors, and the gardens fell into disrepair. "Everything changed once health and safety legislation started to come in; working outside became very difficult. From the 1960s onwards, there was a growing feeling that patients shouldn't be engaged in work, that it was against their human rights. But it went too far – funding and support for work schemes that had been beneficial for people stopped.

"It was the patients who began to say they wanted to get involved in gardening and to be able to roam the grounds. It was then that we decided to take a more co-ordinated

> **Together, we weave through row after row, each one different from the last**

approach. We looked at all the space we had and decided we should be making the most of it. A group of us set about to develop that idea as much as we could."

Today, Bethlem offers a range of outdoor-related occupational therapy work programmes, in gardening, as well as cookery, that make the most of the fresh produce grown on site. Bethlem treats a wide range of people with varying levels of mental health issues: depression, eating disorders, addiction, schizophrenia and self-harm. For those not able to engage in the occupational schemes, hospital grounds have been landscaped with nature trails along woodland paths and meadows. These are so popular that a box of leaflets in Peter's offices with information about the walks continually needs refilling.

As Peter has been leading the charge here over the last few years, evidence has begun to emerge that contact with the environment and wildlife play a crucial role in the treatment of mental illness. In 2007, the charity Mind published the results of two studies by the University of Essex that showed that 90% of people who took part in gardening projects, green walks and cycling groups experienced benefits to their mental and physical health, with the combination of nature and exercise the most important factor. Mind now recommends that ecotherapy be included in health and social care budgets. "It is quite hard to get exact evidence, but there is definitely a growing recognition about what the natural world can do for mental well-being," says Peter. "But we do know that there is sensory stimulation from being with the sun and wind; it is good for one's mood."

Patients can learn a horticultural skill and are paid a basic wage for their work. "Through the orchard project and other gardening groups, we are able to engage people in the manual tasks, prepare them for more vocational work and build self esteem. Some have difficulties with desk-based jobs but get on better and feel much more capable working outdoors."

Peter obtained the funding and, just as importantly, the help to clear the site of brambles. He then invited the London Orchard Project to get involved – which donated the skills of orchard expert Bob Lever. With Bob's help, the patients got on with the planting of new trees, researching the varieties on site so that trees of the same provenance could be used, as well as pruning and cutting dead branches away. "We planted just a few new trees initially – apples, plum and greengage – but in the spring just gone we filled in the gaps."

Where rows had been completely destroyed, heritage varieties that were likely to have grown here – such as Laxtons Fortune – were used. "The London Orchard Project was quite excited by what it found here," says Peter. "They had worked on much smaller sites around the city, in wastelands or parks. The chance to do something on this scale was great for them."

Bob and the volunteers were keen to get a spread of trees that would provide fruit throughout the entire harvesting period – August to November. And for good reason. Funding for the project came from the Big Lottery Local Food scheme, which distributes grants to ensure communities can access food grown in their area easily and cheaply. Apples from the orchard are harvested and used by the cooking groups run in the hospital's therapy kitchen. Plans are afoot to publish their recipes in a book.

But, thanks to Peter, it isn't all apple pies. The kitchen harvests a range of fresh produce from a new walled garden (the original Victorian walled garden was knocked down to make way for a new secure unit) and the garden is used by patients taking gardening and cooking courses. In the raised beds, patients help to grow courgettes, cabbages, onions, garlic and blueberries.

Peter shows me the glasshouse over by the wall, where peaches and grapefruits are just beginning to swell. The apricot tree is a riot of spring blossom. "Since apricots flower early there aren't the insects to pollinate them, so we pollinate them with paintbrushes. Patients come here to help. It's a lovely task; quiet and repetitive."

> Hospital grounds have been landscaped with nature trails along woodland paths and meadows

This engagement, says Peter, is reminiscent of a time when people not only relied on the land but on each other. Here, the harvest is a key time of year for those undertaking both gardening and cookery. Peter believes that the tactility of being with the soil is beneficial too, explaining that "by nurturing plants, you have a relationship with them, and you can take satisfaction from seeing their progression".

It is another story of old and new, but a simple one, in a place full of complex narratives and lives. For some, nature will never be the answer. But, as an outsider, one cannot help hoping that what has been achieved so far continues to thrive unimpeded, and that the flourishing ecotherapy goes from strength to strength.

Before we say our goodbyes, Peter wants to show me the hospital meadow, which he proudly tells me will be shoulder height with wildflowers come summer. As we wander towards it on a woodland pathway, we pass two patients following one of the trails, stopping by a fallen trunk of an old cherry to let them pass. I turn to look at it, and see a family of tall, strong shoots growing anew from its bark. Just like the old orchard, heading straight and true towards the light.

Fruits of their labour

Photography by Victoria Nightingale. Illustration by Amie Jones

It is hard to imagine that much of the capital's fruit was once grown in market gardens and orchards all around the city.

But late Victorian London flourished with fruit trees, and clues of the city's farming heritage can be spotted in the names of the apples we eat, and in the trees that grow in the capital's streets, parks and back yards.

Merton Joy or Hounslow Wonder were cultivated in south London orchards. The fruit trees that lived during Lewisham's time as a pear-growing region continue to thrive. In Hackney and the north of London are the survivors of once productive market gardens, as the *Common Ground Book of Orchards* describes: "Walk around Dartmouth Park near Highgate in April, and you can see, through the gaps and between the houses, mature pear trees in full bloom."

Maps from the 1890s show the city's orchards grew mainly in large clusters in south London, particularly around Hounslow, Isleworth and Kingston-upon-Thames; a large community of flourishing fruit farms that included Bromley's Bethlem Orchard, which still remains (*see page 92*).

Bethlem is just one of many orchards that has been brought back into use by the London Orchard Project, an organisation dedicated to providing urban fruit to urban communities, and to reversing the fact that the UK now imports 70% of its apples.

The charity has been working around the city since 2009, restoring many old orchards and planting new ones, as well as giving Londoners the opportunity to eat produce grown locally. As Kath Rosen, who runs the organisation, says: "There's no reason not to have thriving fruit trees in the capital."

Among its latest projects are the restoration of a large apple orchard with heritage varieties in Streatham, and a pear and plum orchard in Lewisham. In Ealing, Heathfield Gardens has recently been established with greengage, plum and medlar trees. Some of its projects are open and accessible to the public, including at Claybury Park in Redbridge – a 1920s orchard of 40 trees (for more, see map).

As well as providing vital habitats for bees, bats and birds, fruit from its orchards does not go to waste. After harvesting season, fruit is distributed around the local area through juicing festivals, cider-making workshops or to charities that supply food to those in need. And its harvesting work can be very large-scale too: in autumn 2010, 400kg of fruit was picked and given away as part of a project with Transition Town Stoke Newington.

Kath says the organisation will consider any space: orchards have been created on housing estates, prisons and schools. Sites just need landowner permission, and must not be too shady or overhung with other larger trees. Most of all, it looks for commitment from people who will look after an orchard long-term. Training is provided for orchard leaders, and in skills such as pruning to help volunteers to keep the orchards healthy.

The charity works with both heritage and newer varieties to bring an orchard to life. Cellini apple, developed in Vauxhall, has been planted in parks nearby such as Ruskin Park, while Hounslow Joy has been planted at Feltham Young Offenders' Institution. "We also plant things that capture the imagination; Winter Banana apple taste like banana, and Pitmaston Pineapple tastes of pineapple. Children love them!" says Kath.

"London has a strong fruit-growing heritage and we introduce locally developed varieties back into orchards as well as balancing that with more hardy varieties that are able to resist diseases," she adds.

See the organisation's top ten recommended orchards on the map (right).

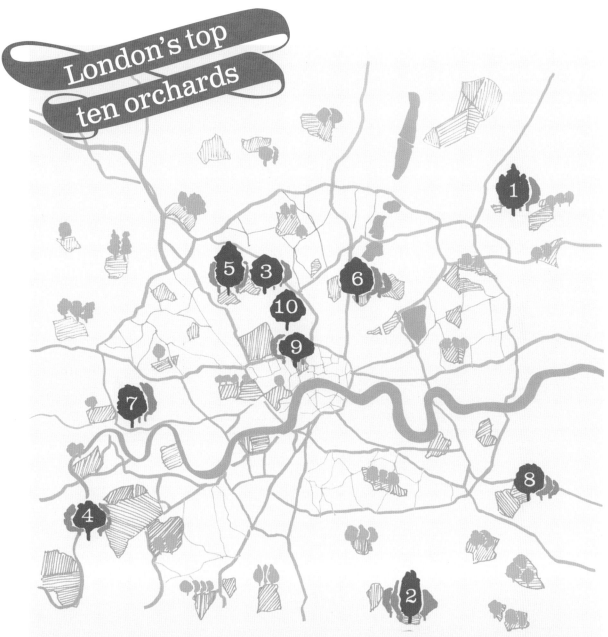

London's top ten orchards

1 Claybury Park, Redbridge – open access. 1920s orchard of around 40 trees in the park, with stunning views across London

2 Bethlem Royal Mental Hospital, Bromley – by appointment. 1920s orchard of more than 200 trees

3 La Sainte Union School, Kentish Town – by appointment with the school. Stunning orchard of apples and heritage espaliers

4 St Michael's Convent Orchard, Ham – by appointment or on Open Gardens Days. Beautiful orchard in convent's grounds

5 Fenton House, a National Trust property, Windmill Hill, Hampstead – beautiful walled garden with a 300-year-old orchard

6 Beckers Estate, Hackney – example of a very urban orchard where the microclimate has been used to allow apricots, apples and pears to thrive

7 Heathfield Gardens, Ealing – 17 fruit trees, including some large standard trees, rarely seen in urban orchards, as well as fruits such as greengage, plum and medlar

8 University of Greenwich, Avery Hill Campus, Eltham – large orchard in the grounds of the campus, including apples, pears and mulberry. The university has recently been voted as most green in the UK

9 Alara Wholefoods permaculture orchard, King's Cross – linear orchard in very urban setting, alongside railway sidings in the heart of King's Cross

10 Green Peppers Orchard at Maiden Lane Community Centre, Camden – small mature orchard at Maiden Lane Community Centre restored between 1999 and 2001 by local people

Width limit

2.2m
7.0

Nurturing nature

Words by Lucy Scott. Illustrations by Grace Lee

Tony is an embarrassment to his wife at the supermarket.

Whenever they go, he insists on taking his camera, and spends a long time crouched on the ground snapping pictures of the car parking bays, while his wife fetches the trolley, pretending not to know him. Tony has no interest in the concrete as such, but the little saplings planted there – the kind that those in the know call "lollipop trees". These days his wife just leaves him to it, and does the shopping herself.

Tony Kirkham, the charismatic head of the arboretum at Kew Gardens, tells us that although he is happy he manages to avoid the shopping these days, what he sees in his photographs does not make him happy in the slightest. He flicks through a catalogue of his findings on a projector for the 400-strong audience that is gathered at Kew Gardens today to celebrate the first birthday of the Londoners Love Trees initiative, and tells us that it is not only supermarket car parks that are to blame.

He shows us slide after slide of doomed, stunted specimens hemmed in to tiny patches of soil. Their skinny trunks and rounded crowns (hence their nickname) are constrained on either side by the straps that tie them to rigid stakes, and from below – leaving them no space to spread their roots. These lollipops are so endemic in the city that landscape architects, botanists, arboriculturalists and anyone who cares about urban trees are extremely worried about what's in store for London in years to come.

> Most of our finest urban trees are a legacy of the 19th century, a response to a time when the railways and factories of the Industrial Revolution covered the city's skies with smoke

Tony shows us more pictures to highlight his concerns; in particular, a pair of images of the Palace of Westminster, as seen from Parliament Square. One is recent, and shows a line of aged, hefty London plane trees lining the vista, sheltering the people sitting on the common from the traffic as it zooms around the roundabout behind. The other depicts the same view, but without the trees. All that remain are buildings and traffic – a barren, stark, depressing, treeless landscape.

As cities go, London's streets boast substantial tree cover – largely thanks to the Victorians. Most of our finest urban trees are a legacy of the 19th century, a response to a time when the railways and factories of the Industrial Revolution filled the city's skies with smoke, and turned the Thames and other rivers into open sewers. Organisations such as the Royal Society for the Protection of Birds (RSPB), the National Trust and the Commons Preservation Society emerged in an effort to protect the natural city, while the middle classes began to plant parks and gardens. In an attempt to combat serious air pollution, trees were given the room they needed to thrive; so much so that their plantings define the city today – from stately London planes in parks such as Brunswick Square, to the avenue of London planes that line the Embankment. The only problem is, those trees are now nearing the end of their lives, and the legacy of the current generation of tree planting is not expected to be as successful or long-lasting.

Tony's pictures demonstrate that people in charge of planting trees have scant knowledge about what trees really need to grow, and have failed to grasp the art of planting the right tree in the right location and providing the necessary aftercare. He recalls a particularly distressing example of a line of 100 London plane trees planted in 2005 at a high cost to the public purse. Unwatered during drought and left to fend for themselves, the trees died within the first year, and lessons were not learned. The process was repeated twice more with the same species of tree, in the same spot, with the same lack of aftercare. Just a quarter of that third attempt survives today.

But ignorance is not the only problem. Large trees have a fairly hard time these days because of a variety of well-entrenched misconceptions and/or short-term thinking. The preference in streets is now for smaller, ornamental varieties, for fear that large trees can cause structural damage and pose subsidence risk to buildings – a risk that has been grossly overblown, and led to unnecessary street tree loss in recent years, government research shows.

Keep an eye out for the little ones

After a young tree is planted, there are still a range of tasks that need to be undertaken to ensure the sapling survives. Research has shown that half of newly planted trees die within their first five years because of a lack of aftercare. However, between March and September for the first five years of a tree's life, there are a few tasks that you can perform to help it to survive. Lack of water is one of the biggest problems, particularly if the tree has to compete with surrounding grass. As well as providing it with a drink now and then, check that the guard around the tree is intact and that it is protecting the tree properly. Placing bark chippings around the base will also help to keep it free of weeds.

Does the tree look like it needs water?

As street trees are surrounded by concrete, they find it hard to get all the water they need, and dehydration is a big problem. Fill a watering can every two weeks and give your local street tree a good drink – you'll make its life much easier. Pour the water down the plastic tube, if there is one, which you will find poking out of the soil near the trunk (below, left).

Does the tree need its ties loosening?

When young saplings are planted they are rigged up with small straps to secure them to the stakes that give them support. As the trees get bigger, the straps can become tight and start to strangle the tree.

If the tree is really suffering, the bark may look wounded or scarred, or its trunk may be bulging around the strap. Check to see if the straps are rubbing or chafing the bark and that the guard is still effective. Simply taking a few seconds to loosen the straps could save the tree's life.

The straps might need to be removed altogether, but make sure you seek permission from the owner before you take the scissors to it.

Do weeds need clearing?

Clearing all weeds and grasses from around the base of the tree will ensure that the mulching is still effective.

A report published by the London Assembly in 2007 revealed that around 2,000 London street trees had been cut in the preceding five years, following unwarranted subsidence claims. And although large trees in urban areas are recognised in national and local planning policy, it is usually impossible to incorporate them into new developments because the layout or services are not designed to accommodate them. Developers generally do not like to make space for trees, and lighting, signage and CCTV cameras often take precedence in architectural designs.

But the audience at Kew Gardens might be able to make a difference. Today, Tony has the devoted attention of volunteers who have recently been taking part in a training programme to teach skills in planting, growing, surveying and caring for urban trees – a scheme provided by the Tree Council and Trees for Cities, supported by the London Tree Officers Association and Barcham Trees, and funded by the mayor of London. They aim to enlist 4,000 city dwellers, with a wide range of ambitions: from contributing to community tree-planting sessions on the odd weekend, to training in urban forestry and more formal roles as part of a city-wide network of Tree Wardens – who act as the eyes and ears for street trees on their doorsteps. The scheme is open to anyone.

As we break for coffee, I start to discuss the slides with a couple named Ian and Jane, and their young daughter, who are sitting near me. They live in Clapham, and have been volunteering for 18 months.

"We took part in the tree plantings recently on Clapham Common, and now we walk past these trees every day on our way to work," says Ian. "It's rewarding to see what we've done and see that others are able to enjoy them too. It totally changes your mood as you pass them. So I can't imagine London without trees – those photos of Parliament Square seem impossible."

But, as we later learn, while photographs of leafy streets such as Holborn's Kingsway turning to a bland highway packs an aesthetic punch, aesthetics is only half the story. "These trees in Kingsway will be disappearing around the time that the effects of climate change begin to hit the city," says Jim Smith, the Forest Commission England's urban forestry adviser, who is next on stage. "Walking down that street on a hot day will be fairly unbearable."

As understanding of climate change increases, there is growing evidence to suggest that bolstering the number and size of our trees will be crucial to making cities like London more hospitable over the next few decades. Jim

is a keen supporter of the recommendations of "No Trees, No Future" – a report that, among other things, urges local authorities to ensure provision is made for large trees in the early stages of a new development. Urban trees reduce the "urban heat island effect", thereby helping to negate the higher temperatures in cities, compared with their surroundings. It is thought that on a hot summer day, central London is nine degrees warmer than its rural hinterland. The trees also provide shade, remove dust and particulates from the air, and even help to reduce traffic noise by absorbing and deflecting sound.

"Temperatures in our cities are likely to become more difficult to live with as the effects of climate change increase," says Jim.

After Jim leaves the stage, Tony leads the volunteers into the sunshine for a tour of Kew Gardens. Our first stop is by the garden's Lucombe oak, planted at Kew in 1773 and now as wide as a house. It used to live 20 metres away, in the middle of a pathway that was to become Syon Vista – now an avenue of lusty holm oaks that still runs more than 1,000 metres west to the Thames. By the time landscape architects came to create the avenue in 1845, the great oak was 72 years old. Rather than fell it, they gently moved it to the side.

The Victorians had the right idea.

The sky's the limit

A few days later, I head to Lambeth's Garden Museum for their Trouble with Trees event, where landscape architect Brita von Schoenaich expresses her frustration with "the orthodoxies of architects and developers".

"The whole system is against planting large trees in London," she says. But she is optimistic that we now have the technology to "recreate what was once there".

She is, of course, referring to woodlands, and shows us a diagram that outlines the change in tree cover across London, from Roman times to the present day. It is a story of gradual loss, up until the last picture, dated now, which shows a tree atop a skyscraper.

The concept of growing forests in the sky – which enable office workers to escape into a woodland world of mulch, leaves and bark by taking a lift to the top of their buildings – currently exists on the fringes of architectural responses to space constraints in cities. Brita and Christopher Bradley-Hole proposed such a scheme for Fenchurch Street in 2006. At the time, the planners were unnerved by the unpredictability of nature, and how the leaves shed might impact on the built environment.

> Large species trees are key to creating climate-proof, happy and healthy cities

But just a few years later in Milan, a tower that hosts the world's first vertical forest – with trees on every balcony – is rising into the skyline.

I am sitting next to Tom Armour, leader of the landscape architecture group at Arup, which in 2012 published a report outlining the economic benefits of urban tree planting. Tom says the growing evidence of the cost benefits of trees will mean schemes like Brita's could become more mainstream in years to come.

Work is now under way in London to provide a cost-benefit analysis for trees, following studies undertaken in New York. The U.S. study showed $1 spent on trees each year generates $5 in quantifiable benefits – increasing property prices, reducing energy consumption by regulating local microclimates, improving physical and mental health and reducing hospital recovery times, as well as increasing workplace productivity. The New York City Parks Department recently determined that the 600,000 street trees in its five boroughs provide an annual benefit of more than $100m – more than five times what it costs to maintain them.

"Cities are beginning to recognise and measure the value of their existing large species trees," says Tom. "The evidence shows that they are key to creating climate-proof, happy and healthy cities for the future. So why aren't we planting more large trees instead of the small 'lollipop' species you see being planted along city streets today?"

Shining specimens

Back in the classroom, it's "tree ID" night with Jon and Margaret from the Tree Council, at their offices just near London Bridge – another aspect of the Londoners Love Trees training programme.

Jon, a botanist and programme director of the scheme, hands some leaves around to his students. They hold their specimens up to the light, and ponder. There are shrugs of shoulders all round, as few of us are sure we know the name of the leaf we are holding. The man in front of me looks quizzically at a branch of ginkgo biloba, with its exotic and uniquely fan-shaped leaves. As he confers with his neighbour, my quiet satisfaction at knowing what he's holding is snuffed out when Jon hands me a cutting with oval-shaped leaves I recognise but cannot identify. We all love trees. But we are all hopeless at this.

Later, we head out into the nearby park just before dusk, to put what we've learned to use, clutching vintage tree books we've been given as a guide. On the curbside, opposite the entrance to the park, I stop under a grand old common lime tree, gently pull one of its slender branches towards me, and peer closely at its greenish-yellow leaves, oblivious to the cars as they pass.

London's trees

Common beech
Fagus sylvatica
Type of seed: **Nut**

Hazel
Corylus avellana
Type of seed: **Nut**

Sycamore
Acer pseudoplatanus
Type of seed: **Winged seed**

Yew
Taxus baccata
Type of seed: **Fleshy fruit**

Rowan
Sorbus aucuparia
Type of seed: **Fleshy fruit**

Common alder
Alnus glutinosa
Type of seed: **Cone**

Kew's treetop walk (South-west)

Hanging out in the treetops is a perspective on the natural world that usually only arborists can enjoy. But Kew Gardens' treetop walk unlocks that pleasure to all.

This walkway enables visitors to journey through the canopy of mature broad-leaved trees that form the Capability Brown–designed woodland area at the gardens, which was introduced to demonstrate the importance of trees for wildlife, the climate, and the biodiversity of the forest canopy.

Tawny owl, woodpecker, and kestrel can be viewed up close, and visitors can catch a glimpse of species that rarely venture onto the woodland floor, such as the purple hairstreak butterfly. The walkway is open all year around, so walkers can see the effects of the seasons on trees, just as the birds might.

A spectacular example is the northern red oak, whose leaves turn a deep red in autumn. It doesn't fare well in cities, as it needs plenty of space for its broad crowns, so the Kew walkway offers a rare chance to see this colourful display in London. At other times of the year, it can be identified by its leaf shape. While it still has the basic lobes synonymous with the English oak, its lobes are pointed.

In the summer months, walkers can see the masses of catkins produced at the upper reaches of the sweet chestnut tree, while the silver lime produces yellow flowers that give off an intoxicating scent of lilies – a scent just barely discernible down on the woodland floor. If you are up there on a windy day, you will see why this tree was introduced to Britain for its beauty. When the leaves are disturbed by the wind they reveal their silvery undersides, which contrast sharply with their green upper surfaces, making the tree look as though it is shimmering with silver.

Through the year

In spring, a tapestry of many shapes of leaves, all with differing shades of green, returns to the woodland canopy. A woodpigeon forages for the sugary sap of horse chestnut flowers.

In late July, bees venture into the treetops searching for nectar, and feed on the yellow flowers of the silver lime. Leaves broaden with the sunlight, and dense bunches of flowers adorn the crowns. In the bark of a dead tree, woodpeckers are busy searching for insects.

Acorns mature in the mossy cups of the Turkey oaks come autumn. The spiny fruits of the horse chestnut fall to the ground and split to reveal shiny conkers. Winter is bare, but with the leaves gone, the woodland's urban context comes to the fore with the arch of Wembley Stadium clearly visible on the horizon.

Getting there

Kew Gardens is a few minutes' walk from Kew Gardens Station, which is served by the District Line and London Overground. But cycling or walking there along the Thames Path is much more fun.

The Thames Path is a national trail that runs 180 miles along the banks of the River Thames, and runs along the far side of the gardens.

The gardens can be accessed from this path at the Brentford Gate, where bicycle racks are available. You can also take a riverboat service, which runs between April and October. Boats leave a few times daily from Westminster Pier.

A lift is available at the bottom of the walkway for disabled and mobility-impaired visitors.

Nearby natural wonders

Once you have descended back to earth from the treetop canopy, head to Kew's Palm House and take the 1,200-metre walk along the Syon Vista towards the River Thames. The broad grassy avenue, framed by holm oaks, was one of three vistas planted in 1845-46, to encourage the public to venture into the arboretum. The view of Syon House, the Duke of Northumberland's London home, is also visible, and there is plenty more to catch the eye along the way.

The lake stretches for more than half the length of the walk itself, and is the perfect place to take a book and a picnic. Lie in the long grass by the banks, as ducks and geese waddle past. And if you do make it to the end, head into the conservation area — a raw, wild patch of woodland grown entirely for the benefit of wildlife. Keep an eye out for gigantic nettles, as well as bluebells.

Great spotted woodpecker
Spends most of its time clinging to tree trunks and branches. Woodlands, especially with mature broad-leaved trees, are its favoured habitat.

Silver lime
A striking, statuesque tree from eastern Europe. Bees pollinate the flowers but die in the process as the nectar is toxic to them.

Nuthatch
Best looked for in mature woods and established parkland, on the sides of tree trunks and the undersides of branches.

Seeds of change

As spoken by Mihaly Herczeg. Photography by Micha Theiner

The English love their tomatoes, and so do I. I love the smell that the vines give off when you brush past or give them water: it's almost as though they're trying to communicate with you. And I love eating them in a fry-up, something I've learned to do since moving to England eight years ago. But in the grey London climate, a decent and tasty harvest of your own is hard to achieve, which is why I created Tomato World on a small nursery site in Greenwich.

I come from a long line of Hungarian farmers, so you could say farming is in my blood. Yet when I left my dairy farm and my sheep and came to London, I lost that part of my life. During my first few years here, I made my living working on construction sites, building houses and converting lofts. But I soon started to miss the rural existence, and so I began to look for ways to have it again in the city.

It's not easy to be a farmer in London, and my wife and I spent a long time searching for the right home. Eventually we found a little spot near Woodlands Farm in Shooters Hill: a bungalow with a garden, a small brook and, behind it, 2 hectares of wasteland overgrown with blackberry bushes.

We bought a rotavator and began cultivating it — cutting back the bushes, tilling the soil and working hard to turn the plot into a productive space. The land and the climate in London are so different from back home. Hungary is flat and sunny, and so we had to learn new ways of working with this new landscape.

The soil on our plot has a lot of clay, so it's hard to grow things directly in the earth: it can get clogged with water, making it difficult for air to get to the plants' roots. So we got round this by laying half of the land with compost and layer upon layer of woodchip, as a base for growing produce in pots instead. On the other half, we planted a meadow and bought two friendly chestnut mare horses for grazing.

Just a few years on and our small farm is a productive nursery site where we grow plants, herbs and trees such as eucalyptus and silver birch, which we sell most weeks at farmers' markets in Clapham, Brixton and Bermondsey.

However, most of our time has been spent building Tomato World. Last summer we grew more than 5,000 plants from 50 different varieties of tomato from all over the world.

Tomato plants are hard to grow in London, mainly because they need a lot of sunshine. Some varieties require up to 120 days a year to ripen and produce good-flavoured fruits. Hearing people tell woeful stories of how they tried in vain to grow these plants, we began experimenting to find the varieties best suited to the city's wet climate.

Londoners often buy 'Moneymaker' seeds, but these are not suited to the weather and grow up to a metre in height, which is no good for balconies and window sills. Some other varieties are only suited to polytunnels, which Londoners tend not to own.

However, there are a few varieties that we've found work well in the city, after growing the same type of plant year after year to test them out. The Hungarian variety 'Cherolla' is fantastic for balcony boxes and kitchen gardens; it's also productive, with fruit that grows in clusters and that's ideal for eating fresh in salads.

There are a few varieties we've found work well in the city

'Goldkrone', also from Hungary, has yellow fruit and does well in vegetable pots or balconies. The Romanian variety 'Marmande' is ideally suited to small spaces, and tastes great when pickled. The 'Elan' variety, also from Hungary, can resist London's lower spring temperatures, but you'll need a garden to grow it.

To get the most out of your plants, keep them warm in spring and not too hot in summer. Chilly temperatures slow their growth, while sizzling summer days can cause the flowers to drop off. Don't overfeed them with too much nitrogen, and make sure that you pluck all the first flowers; that way, it won't devote too much energy to forming fruit before its roots and foliage have filled out.

With Tomato World up and running, we have now opened our first shop. Dig This Nursery (*pictured*) is a small garden centre tacked on to the side of a pub opposite New Cross Gate Station, which specialises in plants and herbs for small spaces. I used to buy my Christmas trees from a shop next to the pub, and for this reason I would always glance towards it as I drove past. One day I went by and saw that the shop had disappeared, and that no one was using the space. I parked my car and went to speak to the pub landlord about renting it. We shook hands, did a deal, and the next day my son and I began building the shop from scratch together.

For more tomato tips from Mihaly Herczeg, go to digthisnursery.co.uk

Life in an ancient woodland

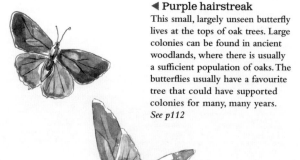

◀ **Purple hairstreak**
This small, largely unseen butterfly lives at the tops of oak trees. Large colonies can be found in ancient woodlands, where there is usually a sufficient population of oaks. The butterflies usually have a favourite tree that could have supported colonies for many, many years.
See p112

Few kinds of woodland are as rich in life as an ancient wood because the older the woodland, the more species it tends to support.

The species that indicate that a woodland is ancient vary from one geography to the next – even across a small area such as the UK – but generally plants that thrive in these spots are those that rely on the stability a long-term woodland provides. So they might have poor ability to disperse, have short-lived seed banks or are well adapted to deep shade.

Ancient woodland, which was the original habitat of much of London, is land that has been continuously wooded since at least around 1600: it was 400 years ago that the first known maps were drawn up, and the first widespread tree plantings took place – which means anything in existence at that time was almost certainly natural in composition. Some sites could even link back to the original Wildwood that covered Britain around 10,000 years ago, just after the last Ice Age.

The city still retains many of these natural wonders, as almost half of the woodland that covers Greater London is ancient. In London and the south-east, telltale signs would include yellow archangel, chaffweed, wood anemone, wood spurge,

bluebell or hornbeam. The presence of hole-nesting birds, such as woodpeckers, pied flycatchers and redstarts, may also suggest ancient lineage.

As they are home to many species of flora and fauna, these London woodlands are beautifully rich throughout the year too. In the spring, bluebells will spread the forest floor with blue, sometimes with millions of flowers, as in Perivale Wood (*see p110*), while drifts of wood anemone provide a springtime cabaret in Queen's Wood, in Muswell Hill.

They can also be interesting places for foragers, who may find ramsons (or wild garlic, as it is also known) in spring. The berries of the wild service tree – another loyal patron of ancient woodlands – steeped in whisky and sugar for a couple of months will turn into a very pleasing alcoholic drink, a bit like sloe gin.

▼ **Black beetle**
Old trees provide an amazing array of microhabitats. Many of the invertebrates found there have very specific requirements and are not found anywhere else. The small black beetle lives inside hollow beeches, in the fruiting bodies of the bracket fungus.

◄ Redstart
Though rarely seen
in London, the redstart
likes the large trees
the ancient woodland
provides, as do other
hole-nesting birds.

▼ Acorns
Acorns provide food for
woodpigeons, rooks, grey
squirrels and mice.

► Old trees
The great age of many of the
trees and their resultant large, thick,
cracked, fissured bark and rot-holes,
all provide numerous additional
microhabitats for other species.

▼ Wood anemone
One of the surest signs of ancient woodland
is wood anemone. Its seed is rarely fertile, and
when it is, it does not stay that way for long.
The plant spreads very slowly, at a rate of 6
feet every hundred years. The stability of the
ancient woodland gives it the conditions
it needs to spread.

Best for bluebells

Perivale Wood (West)

The nature notes handed out at the entrance to Perivale Wood tell you that there are four million bluebells in this 10-hectare nature reserve in Ealing.

At first you think it must be an exaggeration. Then you step into this wonderland and realise there is little reason to doubt or need to try counting for yourself; all that matters is that the bluebells here are one of the city's rare and unforgettable natural sights.

So precious is the wildlife here that Perivale opens to the public just once a year, on either the last Sunday in April, or the first Sunday in May, just in time to see the bluebells in their full glory.

As you venture into their midst, you feel like a trespasser in another land. This is not a place for man, but an ecosystem for ever-increasing numbers of

butterfly, moth and bird species that have made this reserve home – where the long meadow grass provides habitat for lizards and butterflies, while the shaded waters of the medieval pond shelter the smooth newt and woodland birds.

Perivale, also known as Braddish Wood, is 7 hectares of ancient woodland, and almost one of recent habitat, while meadow, pasture and scrubland are grazed by four horses from May to October, to maintain an untidy sward and edge. Before machinery, fertilisers and tidying up of farms, this is how many a UK pasture would have looked.

The old-school style of management, employed today on this patch of old Middlesex, is down to the commitment of the Selborne Society, which purchased the site in 1923. It was the culmination of efforts begun some years earlier by one of its members, Robert Read – an Ealing naturalist, who had fallen in love with the birdsong he had heard coming from the wood as he worked along the nearby Grand Union Canal.

Read pioneered a project to protect birds in the area, and as early as 1902 Perivale was established as a bird sanctuary, and a keeper employed to protect the woodland against poachers, bird-catchers, egg collectors and flower sellers who had long regarded it as a free hunting ground.

When the society acquired the site, the surrounding area was a rural idyll. Although the expanding city has made its way here, the contours of this nature reserve have remained largely the same for the best part of 250 years – perhaps even longer. So, what you may glimpse here but once a year is a rebellion against that urban march.

Through the year

As the woodland awakes, springtime blossom erupts from the wild service and blackthorn trees and the floor is awash with bluebells, before May brings the gold tones of the yellow archangel. Vines and brambles creep across the forest floor. The tree canopy thickens above, and so dense is the vegetation that visibility is reduced to a few meters. Small brown butterflies are spotted in rare dapples of light.

In summer, the long grass of the ancient pasture hosts legless lizards and small brown field voles, while ringlets, marbled white and brown argus feast on flora in the north paddock. The air is filled with honeysuckle perfume.

Little orange wood mice swarm over the boughs of the ancient trees as autumn comes, but are soon preyed on by the tawny owls that lurk in the trees.

Winter beats the woodland into retreat, as animals and plants batten down the hatches. But the odd long-tailed tit and goldcrest can be seen venturing across frosted ground, to feed on the fruits of the oak, hazel, hawthorn and holly.

Getting there

Perivale is a few minutes' walk from Perivale Station, served by the Central Line. The surrounding area belongs to section nine of the Capital Ring Walk, which follows the Grand Union Canal towpath on one side of the site, from the nearby Paradise Fields Wetlands nature reserve.

Nearby natural wonders

Paradise Fields Wetlands was created on the site of the former Greenford Golf Course and has established itself as a wildlife haven. It is now managed primarily for nature conservation and comprises reedbeds, wetland areas and hay meadows. Many rare bird species nest here, including reed buntings and several species of warbler. A pair of lapwing has bred in recent years – a rare occurrence in Greater London.

At 275 metres, nearby Horsenden Hill is one of the finest natural viewpoints in London and a popular kite-flying spot. On a clear day, the Chiltern Hills are visible to the west.

Hawthorn
Well known as a hedgerow plant, uncut hawthorn grows into large trees. Their berry-like fruits are the perfect meal for thrushes, like the blackbird and fieldfare.

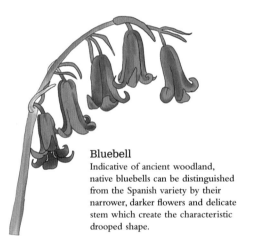

Bluebell
Indicative of ancient woodland, native bluebells can be distinguished from the Spanish variety by their narrower, darker flowers and delicate stem which create the characteristic drooped shape.

Elephant hawk-moth
A medium-sized hawk moth, on the wing from May to July. Common in woodlands, where it can be seen at dusk.

Flight of fancy

Words by Richard Jones. Illustrations by Natalie Mosquera

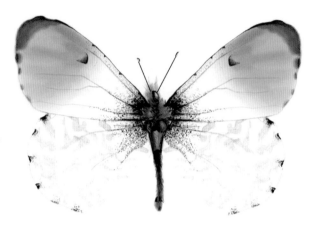

Everyone loves butterflies. With their bright colours, their ephemeral delicacy, their sometimes slow-flapping, sometimes wild erratic flight, and their associations with sunshine and lazy summer days, what's not to love? It is easy to forget, though, that behind every butterfly lies something that is hidden and secret, yet mundanely prosaic. Behind every butterfly is a caterpillar.

Slow, camouflaged and little more than cylindrical plant-eating machines, caterpillars are often overlooked, but since it is the long-lived caterpillar that does most of the feeding, and certainly all of the growing, it is this humdrum earth-bound stage in the life cycle that is arguably much more important than the short-lived aerial imp of an adult. It is by looking at the lives of the caterpillars that we can truly get a feel for three of London's most distinctive and charismatic butterflies.

The holly blue, *Celastrina argiolus*, immediately distinctive because of its powder-blue undersides, could quite equally be called the "ivy blue". Uniquely among British butterflies, the holly blue goes through two generations a year, each feeding on a completely different food-plant. Adults emerging from their chrysalides in April lay their eggs on the unopened flower buds of holly trees, and the dumpy turquoise caterpillars spend a month or so feeding on the developing berries. They eventually give rise to a summer-flying generation of adults in July and August that lay their eggs on the buds of ivy flowers. These caterpillars feed through to October, then make their squat brown pupae in the ivy thatch and wait until spring to start the process all over again.

Being evergreens used to dark shady woods, holly and ivy grow widely in small overshadowed gardens. Consequently, the holly blue is the most urban of all butterflies and occurs right into the heart of the capital. There are sightings from deep in Waterloo, Lambeth, Westminster, Holborn and the City. It can turn up anywhere.

And if holly and ivy are not available, London holly blues have made several food-plant swaps and are now found feeding on the buds of firethorn, snowberry, dogwood and spindle. They are not always abundant, though. Holly blues suffer regular cyclical population crashes about every five years, because of a parasitic wasp, *Listrodomus nycthemerus*, that lays its eggs in the caterpillars, killing them. After a crash, the wasps cannot find any more caterpillars to parasitise, so their numbers plummet too, allowing the butterfly to increase again. By all accounts, 2012 was just at the height of holly blue abundance, so expect a dearth of these pretty butterflies soon, but only for a short while.

The orange-tip, *Anthocharis cardamines*, has always been a true herald of spring. In London the main flight is in late April and May, but in 2012 they began to appear in the last week of March due to the unseasonably warm weather. The orange-tipped males in particular are striking in their regular patrol flights, up and down hedgerows or woodland edges, looking for the green-mottled and orange-free females resting in the herbage.

Egg-laying is a slow and precise business, as prominent, isolated unshaded heads of ladies' smock (cuckoo flower) or garlic mustard are examined. Only a single egg is laid on each plant because the hatchling larvae are cannibalistic. The narrow green caterpillars first burrow into flowers, but eventually they will feed only on the long narrow green seed pods, against which they are perfectly camouflaged.

As they feed, the caterpillars sequester chemicals from the bitter mustard oils in their food-plants (these are relatives of cabbage, whose leaves are similarly unpalatable to humans unless cooked). Throughout the miraculous transformation into chrysalis, then butterfly, the poisonous chemicals are retained, and the white of the adult butterfly, with or without the added orange flash of the males, is a warning

to birds that they taste foul.

The damp woodland and hedgerow habitat of the orange-tip's food-plants means that the butterfly is less likely to be seen in dense inner London, and avoids the more well-tended ornamental parks, but it is quite at home in the large gardens of the Victorian housing boom, where wild shady places abound. It seems to avoid the East End, but ranges from 4 o'clock to 1 on the London clockface, through Greenwich, Dulwich, Streatham, Wandsworth and Barnes, round to Hampstead and Stoke Newington.

The purple hairstreak, *Neozephyrus quercus*, is so easy to miss because, unlike most other butterflies, the adults do not visit flowers to sip nectar. Instead, they settle on leaves covered with the dripped honeydew from aphids. Aphids suck out so much plant sap to extract meagre quantities of protein, that most of the sugary liquid is simply ejected at the other end. It tastes perfectly good to bumblebees, ants and hairstreaks.

In addition, purple hairstreaks lay their eggs on oak trees, and although they will visit low branches, they have a penchant for large prominent trees offering warm egg-laying sites on the sheltered sunny southern side. The small, flat, woodlouse-shaped caterpillars hatch from the eggs in April, coinciding with leaf-burst, and they bind the brown scaly leaves of the developing bud with a loose net of silk. Instead of falling off, the scales are retained and provide the growing caterpillar with a sheltering cocoon, from which it ventures at night to feed on the oak leaves.

Mystery still surrounds the purple hairstreak chrysalis, but there are suggestions that the caterpillar drops from the tree to seek out red-ant nests in which to pupate. In captive-breeding experiments, the caterpillars attract ants by offering sweet secretions

from their bodies, and they are small enough to be carried off back to the nests.

Often only the most extensive gardens have the right combination of large oak trees and suitable ant nests, and the purple hairstreak is mostly a woodland butterfly, frequenting the outer more wooded suburbs from Orpington and Richmond, round to Perivale, Harrow and Southgate.

Nevertheless, a single large oak in Battersea Park has long had its own small colony, and the relic woods in Dulwich, Sydenham and Norwood also support small numbers.

Epping Forest
cycle path

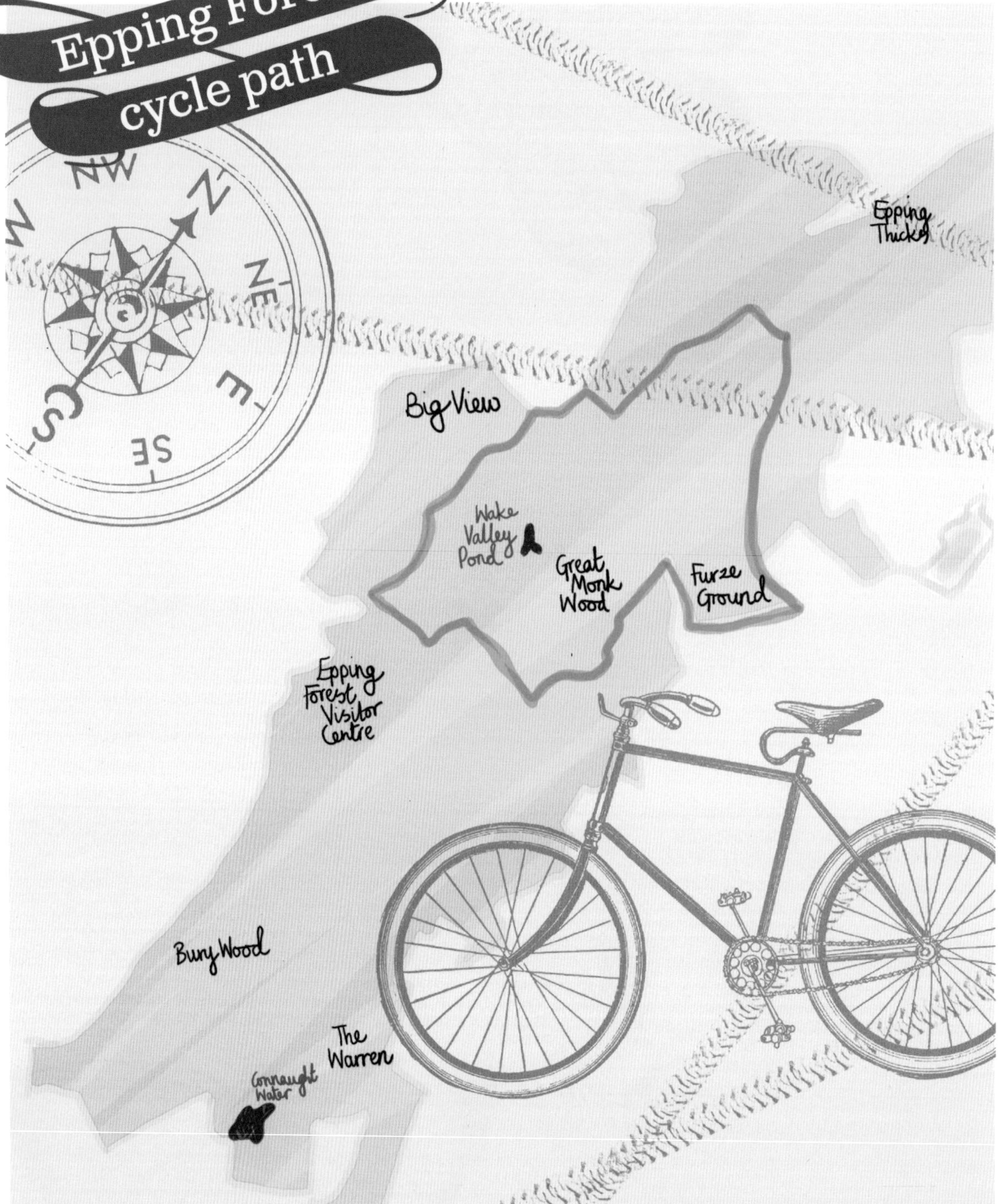

Epping Thicks

Big View

Wake Valley Pond

Great Monk Wood

Furze Ground

Epping Forest Visitor Centre

Bury Wood

The Warren

Connaught Water

Jazz and blues

Words by Lucy Scott

"It's like playing jazz, isn't it?" says the voice from behind us. Andrea and I turn round to see a lady in a red fleece sitting on a bench by the bike track, sipping water from a bottle. Having spotted our confused faces, her guess – that our trip round Epping Forest has been as freeform as a Miles Davis concert – is spot-on.

"Do you have any idea where we are?" I ask, propping my bike on its stand. She heaves herself upright, unfolds her map from its neat concertina and into a large sheet for us to see.

I trace my finger round the green line that marks the route we should have followed, before making an impressionistic squiggle to show where we've actually been. "So ... I think we're all here," she says, putting her finger on the end of a yellow kidney-shaped patch amid the vastness that represents thousands of hectares of ancient woodland. "Do you know Big View?" asks Andrea. "That's where we're heading." "You're the second person who's asked me that today," says the lady. "And I have absolutely no idea."

I am thoroughly disappointed in Andrea. Getting lost is the kind of thing I do, but I had her down as the type of girlfriend who would know how to read a map. She wears high heels to smart meetings and uses City airport for business trips, and I really believed she was the sort of person who, if she needed to stop people to ask for directions, wouldn't just feel warmly grateful for being told, while failing to take in the specifics.

But as we'd been fiddling with the height of our bicycle seats back at base camp, it seems Andrea had recognised exactly what I meant when I warned her I lacked any sense of direction. What I hadn't recognised was that this was a personality trait that we shared, and as we cycled away from the helpful lady in the fleece I realised that our trip was destined to be the opposite of the quick loop of the forest that we'd both anticipated.

Wayne, who runs the cycle hire shop at Debden House campsite, had waved us off with such hope, and it certainly wasn't his fault that we got lost. His instructions had been very clear: written in biro on our A4 map were the names of exotic-sounding places, arrows indicating the directions, and the approximate times that it would take us to get from one beauty spot to the next. Wayne had promised us the sight of a herd of longhorn cattle grazing the open land and "maybe" the prospect of some muntjac deer roaming free.

He'd then drawn a large circle on the map to mark our stop for lunch. That was somewhere near Big View,

a mystical-sounding place in the north-western reaches of the forest, the pursuit of which would come to define the next few hours. I never asked what it was a big view of, being eager to keep up the suspense. I remain in suspense to this day.

"So, which way out of the gate?" I whispered quietly, the moment we disappeared from Wayne's sight. "I don't know," Andrea whispered back, preoccupied with the novelty of her numerous gears. "Didn't he say something about a track and a hill?"

At the junction we'd looked in both directions and, finding neither a track nor a hill, pushed onwards and upwards through a steep lane and into a tunnel of woods. On the other side of a muddy bank to our right we came across the far end of the campsite where, through the open sides of a small marquee edged with bunting, a group of wedding guests were mingling round a fire. Then we spotted one of the younger members of the party wearing pink wellington boots and scouring the stream with a net.

An hour later we stumble upon the same camp, this time on our left. "It must be another site on the other side of the forest," I say. "Yes, and there's the identical twin of that kid," says Andrea, as we breeze past a child in pink wellington boots scouring the stream with a net.

We make our way towards the entrance to a golf course, and ask a man waiting outside if he can give us directions to the Big View. "A big view of what?" he asks. "We don't know," I say, exasperated. "Never heard of it, and I've lived here 20 years."

"Then it's time you got to know your local area!" says Andrea, before we cycle in tandem back to the B172, the road we've been stuck on skirting the woodland's perimeter.

Our time running out, we veer off the main road and into the first opening we see that will take us back into the forest. It doesn't look like an "official" route, and our trainers pay the price as we shove our bikes through a muddied track pockmarked with the prints of horseshoes. We look as though we're trying to move stalled cars. "I'm disappointed in you," I say. "I'm disappointed in you," says Andrea.

"How was it?" asks Wayne when we finally make it back to base through some idyllic sun-streaked woodland paths. "It was great," I say, fresh from a long run downhill that had no need for pedals.

"We learned what it's like to play jazz," says Andrea.

Oxleas Wood (South-east)

Oxleas Wood is a Site of Special Scientific Interest at the foot of Shooters Hill – a favourite haunt among archers during the Middle Ages and, later, highwaymen. But at one of the highest points in the south of London, today it makes a fantastic spot for view-seekers, and sledges once the snow falls.

Oxleas Wood – which derives from the Old English word meaning "pasture for Oxen" – is part of the more substantial woodland that encompasses Jack Wood, Castle Wood and Shepherdleas Wood (which means "pasture for shepherds" in Old English). But it is thought these woodlands may have been continuously wooded for many thousands of years; information boards on the site say that parts of the wood could date back to the end of the last Ice Age.

Whatever its lineage, Oxleas is undoubtedly home to an incredibly complex community of plants and animals that have grown up and evolved together. Breeding birds, such as the tree creeper, nuthatch, woodpecker, chiffchaff and long-tailed tit have made habitats here, along with relative newcomers, such as the ring-necked parakeet.

The woodland is a tangled vista of towering pedunculate oaks, as well as hazel, sweet chestnut and hornbeam. Walkers will also find a healthy scattering of wild service trees, the berries of which can be picked and pocketed. No other London woodland is known to contain such a large population and size range of this tree.

Look out for the characteristic red berries of butcher's broom too, another key indicator of ancient woodland.

Through the year

In spring, bluebell, wood anemone and wood sorrel carpet the woodland floor, while the returning chiffchaff can be seen flitting through trees and shrubs, distinguished by its distinctive tail-wagging movement. Along the streams and ditches are remote sedge, wood sedge and yellow pimpernel, as well as the uncommon Forster's woodrush.

As the weather warms, and the trees fatten with leaves, walkers can picnic in the nearby meadow, which is managed for wildlife. Butterflies flit among meadow buttercups, ox-eye daises, yarrow, and red and white clover. Among the moths recorded at the site are the festoon, oak lutestring and the seraphim.

The wet weather of autumn encourages a wide variety of fungi to the surface and the lower damper slopes support large populations, particularly where there is an undisturbed litter layer. Several locally uncommon species can be found, including tan ear, scarlett brittlegill and zone rosette. Nuthatches are out searching for hazel nuts.

As winter takes hold, small birds find refuge in the trees but the woodland remains rich for foragers; berries from the hawthorn or the wild service tree can still be gathered.

Getting there

For a great day out at any time of year, visit Oxleas Wood as part of a wider exploration of the capital by foot, since the ancient woodland is part of two designated walks in London.

It is the end of section one of the Capital Ring, which begins at the Woolwich Foot Tunnel, next to the river, and the end of section three of the Green Chain Walk, which begins at Bostall Woods. On lazier days, you can take the train to Falconwood, which is served by London Bridge.

Nearby natural wonders

Just south of Oxleas Wood is Eltham Park North and Shepherdleas Wood, which has distant but clear views towards the City of London and west to Crystal Palace. The pond here is home to tame ducks and geese, and a couple of large terrapins that sunbathe there on warm days. Ponds in the wider area also contain palmate newts, one of the rarest native amphibians in London (*see p64*).

The area is a mix of grassland and ancient woodland, and has a meadow that's only mown in late summer, so that butterflies and other insects can feed on wildflowers and flowers, in turn, can set their seed.

Notable tree species are willow, oak, sweet chestnut, ash and holly and there are cowslips in the meadow.

For tips on urban foraging, see p128

Tree creeper
A small, very active, bird that lives in trees. Climbs them by starting at the bottom and working upwards in a spiral around the trunk.

Butcher's broom
Evergreen shrub that bears scarlet berries in winter. Native to old woods and hedgerows.

Wild service tree
A rare British tree that occurs in patches of old woodland of oak and ash. At its best in autumn, when its leaves turn purplish-red. Its fruits can be turned into a great alcoholic tipple.

Tawny townie

Words by Mark James Pearson. Illustration by Alice Potter

Owls are one of the most magical and enigmatic families in Britain's avifauna, a reputation earned not least through their perceived shyness and often secretive habits. Almost all our native owl species are sensitive to disturbance, are associated almost exclusively with more rural habitats, and tend to shun the urban environment that the majority of Londoners call home.

Almost all, that is. The one exception is the tawny owl, a widespread, well-known, intricately plumaged and beautiful native species that has inspired centuries of folklore and the mournful, evocative hooting so essential to horror films (and easily mimicked with cupped hands and practice).

Tawny owls are remarkably tolerant of human disturbance, and have adapted admirably to what are often isolated pockets of suitable habitat in the capital, including some deep within its urban heart; thus tawnies are very much London's owl. Although mixed woodland is where tawny owls traditionally prosper, they are just as likely to set up territories in parks, cemeteries, railway sidings and even rows of back gardens in the city.

Their diet usually consists of small mammals, but they will also take small birds, worms, beetles and other prey, and studies have shown that they can adapt easily according to availability. An urban owl's supper is therefore as likely to be feathered as it is furred. The homestead, meanwhile, is usually a cavity in a tree, be it a natural hole, or a hollow created by a broken or damaged limb. Where choices are limited, tawnies will also take to specially made nest boxes, dreys and even holes in buildings.

By day, they rely on a combination of the right choice of roosting site and their cryptic plumage as camouflage to evade the attentions of other birds and mammals (including *Homo sapiens*). Tawny owls usually choose branches close to and roughly at a right angle to the main trunk of a tree, and favour branches with cover provided by thick foliage, ideally tangles of ivy or other creepers.

Most of the time it works, and trying to find one – even if you know they're close by – can be like searching for the proverbial needle in a haystack. There are, however, a few tactics one can employ to greatly narrow the search.

The two sure-fire ways of connecting with tawnies in London involve first connecting with locals, of both human and avian persuasions. The ideal humans are those in the know, be they birders, park staff and user groups, or random residents with a passion for "their" local owls. Accumulated knowledge of a resident pair or family of tawny owls in a traditional location is invaluable, and staking out known nest holes and favoured roosting spots is much more reliable than endless "blind" searching.

The London Natural History Society and local bird clubs are good places to start, and tagging along with the various free guided walks in the capital can be a great way of enjoying the city's owls. Tawnies can be found throughout both inner and outer London, from the urban sanctuaries of Kensington Gardens and Abney Park Cemetery, to the leafy suburbs of Richmond and Enfield, but local knowledge goes a long way.

> Tawny owls are remarkably tolerant of human disturbance, and have adapted admirably to isolated pockets of suitable habitat in the capital

Avian locals, as in other birds, can often lead you straight to a roosting owl, even if it is initially invisible. A whole range of familiar garden and woodland species, from blue tits and robins to magpies and jays, engage in a collective harrying of an owl discovered dozing peacefully in the daytime, known appropriately enough as mobbing. A relentless, panicked disturbance aimed at a specific area of foliage on closer inspection will often reveal an owl, usually apparently unfazed by the neurotic attention it has attracted.

Tawny owls conduct almost all their business after dark, with activities often beginning around dusk and continuing in fits and starts throughout the night. Occasionally, however, you may come across adults being peculiarly active, noisy and even apparently tame during the day. This will usually mean you are close to the nest or recently fledged chicks, which can be a blessing or a curse, depending on your luck – they are notoriously defensive parents, and a respectful retreat is strongly advised.

Into the woods

Words by Christopher Stocks. Illustrations by Emma Block

London, like most great cities, has more than its fair share of ghosts. Not just the ghosts of people, those millions of Londoners who lived before our time, but also the ghosts of things: of buildings, of streets, rivers, theatres and shops, markets and pleasure gardens, brothels and factories and pubs and murder scenes. Their traces – faint or entirely forgotten – lie beneath the quotidian city whose bustling streets we hurry along today, anxious that we're going to be late for work.

Which is why, I guess, I'm sitting with a busload of boisterous fellow travellers on the top deck of the alluringly named 176 to Penge, lumbering south from Walworth and Camberwell in search of Matthews the Hairyman and the Queen of the Gypsies. To be frank, I'm probably not looking in the right place, and I'm definitely in the wrong century, but what I do know is that they were to be found hereabouts once. As we swoop down Dog Kennel Hill, towards Dulwich Grove and Lordship Lane, the hills of south London rise up ahead. Today they're dominated by the futuristic ziggurats of the 1960s Dawson Heights estate, which floats above a sea of dinky 19th-century terraces, their anaemic brickwork redeemed (today at least) by the lush green foliage of street trees shivering in the wind.

Once upon a time trees covered these hills for as far as the eye could see, long before the waves of little terraces lapped over them, turning the green space grey all the way between Lambeth and Croydon. For these vales and ridges were the site of the Great North Wood, which originally stretched from Selhurst and Streatham all the way north to New Cross. Though most of it has long since disappeared beneath concrete, tile and brick, the Great North Wood has left its traces, like ghosts, behind. Many of them are as insubstantial as names on a map, but there are more corporeal traces too. Some of the names are obvious once you think of them: Norwood, for example, is just an alternative name for the Great North Wood, while Forest Hill speaks for itself. The street names, on the other hand, sound faintly ironic these days – Giles Coppice, Wood Vale, Thorpewood Avenue – yet their origins may have been blandly descriptive.

As for the corporeal traces, an intriguing map produced by the Friends of the Great North Wood in 1996 shows how many small fragments of the original wood there are, albeit in variously modified forms (*see overleaf*). They slipped through the net of 19th-century development mostly by accident: some, such as the tiny Hillcrest Estate Wood near Crystal Palace, survived as a slip of "waste" ground on the inaccessible slopes of a railway tunnel. Others, like Sydenham Hill Wood, were partly incorporated into the large gardens of Victorian villas; combined with Dulwich Wood, this is the largest remaining fragment we have.

It's easy to mourn the decline of the Great North Wood, but even if it had, somehow, survived the 19th century in its entirety, it would hardly have been the untouched natural forest of the popular imagination. For even in the dim and distant past it was never continuous woodland: as early as the Norman conquest it seems to have been confined to the upper slopes of the hills and ridges between Deptford, Streatham and Croydon. Like most (if not all) British woodlands until the early 19th century, it would have been intensively managed, with a patchwork of coppices, timber trees, felled clearings and wood pasture – hardly what most of us are accustomed to thinking of as "woodland" at all. Yet it provided plenty of local employment, offered a rich range of wildlife habitats, and was in many ways a model of what we would now think of as ecologically sustainable land use.

As far back as the 17th century it was being regarded with some nostalgia. In his *Perambulation of Surrey*, written during the 1680s, the great antiquarian John Aubrey recalled it as "a great wood called Norwood, belonging to the Archbishops, wherein was anciently a tree called the Vicar's Oak, where four parishes met as it were a point.

> Once upon a time trees covered these hills for as far as the eye could see, long before the waves of little terraces lapped over them, turning the green space grey all the way between Lambeth and Croydon

It is said to have consisted wholly of oaks, and among them was one that bore mistletoe, which some were so hardy as to cut, for the gain of selling it to the apothecaries of London, leaving a branch of it to sprout out." Aubrey records that when Oliver Cromwell seized the wood from its then owner, the Archbishop of Canterbury, it extended to 830 acres, but that by his time, as a result of the Civil War, "such havoc had been committed in it that it contained only 9,200 oaken pollards and 80 timber trees".

Like Epping Forest, the Great North Wood was the haunt of highwaymen, charcoal burners and gypsies (whose ghosts are commemorated by Gipsy Hill), and in 1668 Samuel Pepys mentions in his diary: "This afternoon my wife and Mercer and Deb went with Pelting to see the Gypsies at Lambeth, and have their fortunes told; but what they did, I did not enquire." The most famous gypsy fortune-teller of all was Margaret Finch, who lived in a conical hut beneath a tree on Gipsy Hill and became known as the Queen of the Gypsies. An engraving of 1739 shows her smoking a clay pipe at the entrance to her hut, crouched on the ground with a dog by her side. She maintained this posture for so long, apparently, that when she died the following year (at the conceivably factitious age of 109), she couldn't be straightened out again and had to be buried in a specially constructed box.

By 1746, the year that John Rocque published his famous (and beautiful) map of London and its surroundings, the Great North Wood was still around 3 miles across at its widest point, and even in 1802 it was wild enough to shelter a hermit with the alarming name of Matthews the Hairyman. But by then its days were numbered. The use of wood for fuel was already in decline, as Londoners switched to cheap coal shipped from Newcastle, but the three other main woodland products – charcoal for iron smelting, bark for tanning and timber for shipbuilding – were subsequently rendered uneconomic by the Industrial Revolution. Charcoal was replaced by coal and wooden ships by iron ones, while industrially produced chemicals proved far cheaper to use for tanning than laboriously cut and processed oak-bark.

This historic shift affected woods and forests the length and breadth of Britain, and its consequences, in the form of overgrown and undermanaged woodland, are still with us today. But the killer blow for the Great North Wood was its proximity to London – first, because of the rapid spread of railways, which enabled people to live much further from their work, and led to an explosion of house-building; and, second, because of the pollution that explosion brought in its wake.

Stripped of its economic value and in the face of enormous population pressure, the surprise is that anything of the Great North Wood survived at all. Fragmentary though its ghosts may be, they're all the more precious for it, both for us and the wildlife that still, against all the odds, inhabits them.

I may not have found the Queen of the Gypsies or Matthews the Hairyman on the 176 to Penge, but it's still a journey well worth making.

Like Epping Forest, the Great North Wood was the haunt of highwaymen, charcoal burners and gypsies

1 **Dulwich & Sydenham Hill Woods and Cox's Walk:** A sessile oak and hornbeam woodland with the greatest variety of wildlife in the locality

2 **Hitherwood:** Tiny fragment of the Dulwich Woods

3 **Dulwich Upper Wood:** A nature reserve with a range of wildlife

4 **One Tree Hill:** Originally the summit of Oak of Honour Wood

5 **Wood Vale:** Oak pollards that once marked the boundary between Camberwell and Lewisham

6 **Eliot Bank & Little Brownings:** A small remnant

7 **Hillcrest Estate Wood:** Hugs the portal of an old railway tunnel

8 **Vicars Oak:** The site of a boundary oak that marked the meeting point of four parishes. Now a roundabout

9 **Beaulieu Heights:** Ancient and recent woodland, with grassy fields

10 **Long Lane Wood:** Old oaks over rough grassland

11 **Grangewood Park:** Supports a colony of purple hairstreaks

12 **Spa Wood:** Recent woodland and formal park

13 **Biggin Wood:** Retains an ancient border of ditch, bank and boundary oak pollards

14 **Convent Wood:** Only descendant of the Stake Pit Coppices

With thanks to Mathew Frith of London Wildlife Trust for his help.

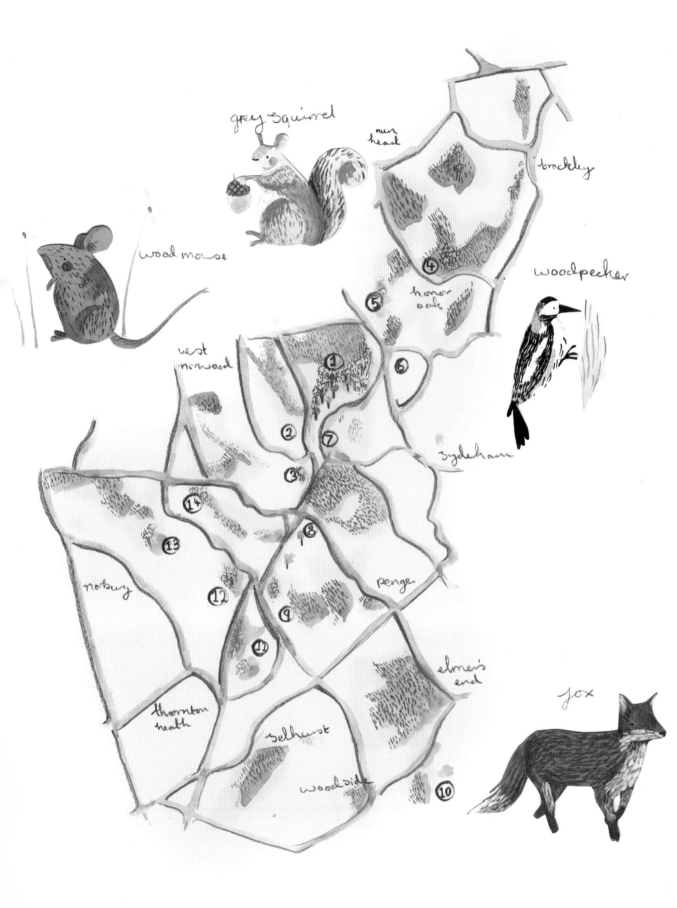

grey squirrel

wood mouse

nun head

brockley

honor oak

woodpecker

west norwood

sydenham

norbuy

penge

elmer's end

thornton heath

selhurst

woodside

fox

A controversial newcomer from America, the grey squirrel is a familiar site across the country, but it is in city spots like Regent's Park where the closest encounters with these cheeky rodents can be experienced.

PHOTOGRAPHY: SAM HOBSON, EDWARD FELTON

When thinking of London
birds, a large green parrot
might not be the first thing
that springs to mind. Yet the
rose-ringed parakeet is now
a common sight, especially
in south-west London.

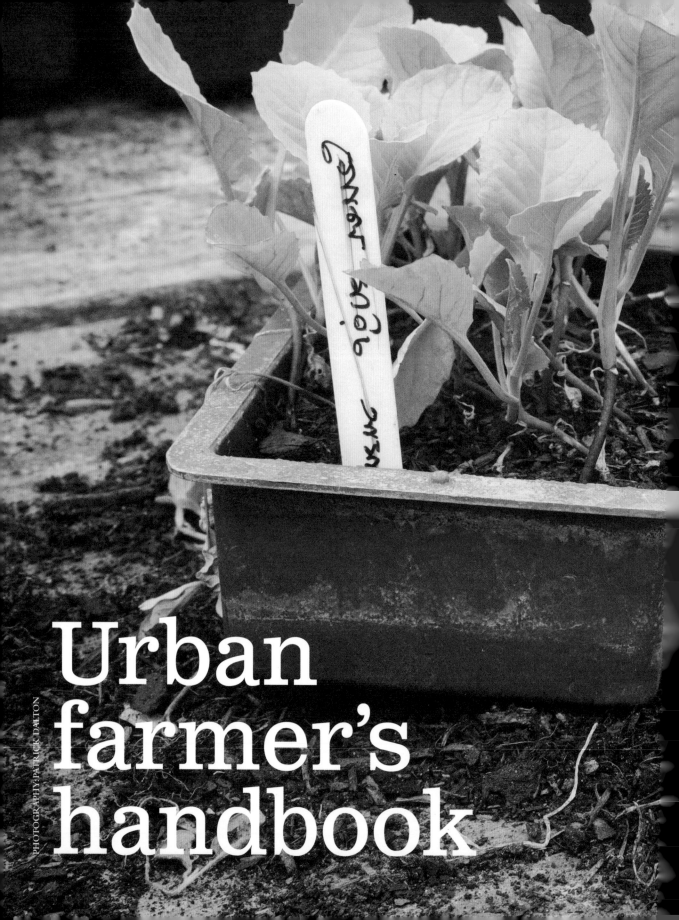

PHOTOGRAPHY PATRICK DALTON

Urban
farmer's
handbook

Forager's guide

Penny Greenhough is not your idea of a typical domestic goddess. A single mum with a complicated past, she lives in a council flat in one of London's less salubrious parts.

But Peckham seen through Penny's eyes is a well-stocked larder that brims with edible bounty. Throughout the year she forages for wild fruits, nuts, leaves and berries.

An alchemist of sorts, Penny transforms her harvest into an array of jams, jellies, chutneys and relishes. In her small kitchen, gleaming glass jars line the surfaces, filled with a rainbow of thick liquids. The cupboards are stuffed with bottles upon bottles of syrups and sauces. Fruits and roots swell, submerged in vodka and gin, while toasted hazelnuts drown in honey and walnuts slowly pickle in vinegar.

Ever eloquent and always inspiring, here Penny describes what motivates her and reveals the tricks of both foraging and preserving. She shares seasonal recipes, inviting you to harvest wild fruits of your own, which you can then transform into treats that are sticky and delicious.

As Penny explains, a kind of self-sufficiency is possible in the city even without a garden or an allotment. She has a simple love of the urban outdoors and a strong desire to see open spaces protected. She believes that to be in these spaces, to witness their moods and to eat what they offer is to get to know them and understand them. For Penny, foraging is a form of appreciation.

Words by Penny Greenhough. Edited by Helen Babbs. Photography by Keiran Perry

Penny's pontack

The saying "by hook or by crook" refers to the ancient right to pick wayside fruit that you could reach from the path with your stick. Since the time of the enclosures in the 18th and 19th centuries – when parliament removed the rights of the people to the casual use of common and uncultivated land – modern developments have encroached on every available space. Even our view of the sky has been appropriated.

Yet even without a garden or allotment, a semblance of self-sufficiency is still possible. I wanted to find a way to demonstrate the value of simple, open spaces and raise awareness of the need to protect them. As an admirer of the English radicals William Cobbett and Thomas Spence, I believe that the nature in our parks and open spaces belongs to us all and should be protected for our use – and foraging is a way of appreciating my surroundings.

Paths are so passé, so why not wander off into the bushes for a while and reclaim the shrubbery? Develop an eye for unlikely spots of interest and derelict or neglected land. Utilise holes in fences if you have to. Try the margins of local playing fields, and the spaces in council estates and churchyards – even public gardens. I figure if no one else is picking it, no one will mind if I do.

Urban areas are often sources of unusual fruit and plants, and we benefit from an extended season because of this. In Peckham, surprising edibles include persimmons and loquats, municipal shrubs like elaegnus and mahonia, and even weirder stuff like the strawberry tree and winter cherry. Spring brings the fresh new leafy growth of hedge garlic, ramsons, wood sorrel, dandelion, wild rocket and nettle. In town, there are vast plantings of rosemary, thyme, fennel and sage.

Elder is a prolific plant that thrives in urban areas and is useful both in flower and fruit form. In spring, use the flowers to make cordial, wine, champagne, tea and fritters. Always pick them on a dry morning and choose only the freshest blossoms – washing will ruin them. A couple of sprays tied in a hankie and chucked in your bath makes a fragrant spring treat after a long winter.

Later on, the berries appear in heavy clusters. They're not for eating raw, and finding something to do with them can be a challenge. Some people swear by elderberry syrup for winter well-being, but one of the most useful things in my cupboard is pontack, a traditional British sauce that's a simple and genuinely tasty way to give elderberries a purpose in life. Pontack is said to take seven years to reach a state of perfection, but you don't have to wait that long. By Christmas you could be using it to enrich stews, casseroles and gravies, or to enliven roasts.

So slow down. Take a deep breath. Notice there is elder all around you on your way home. And make pontack.

Ingredients

* 500g elderberries, de-stalked
* 500ml vinegar
* 200g sugar (optional)
* Two small onions or shallots
* Pinch of salt to taste
* Several blades of mace
* Ground ginger or bruised ginger root
* Small handful of black peppercorns
* A few cloves, allspice berries, ground allspice or pickling spice (you could also add mustard, coriander seed or chilli flakes)

Method

Remove the berries from their stalks using a fork, and rinse them thoroughly under running water. Put the sugar to one side and bung everything else in a non-metallic casserole dish and leave overnight at the bottom of the oven at half a gas mark; I use a slow cooker on low, and just leave the mixture until I get round to it. Next day, strain it through a plastic sieve, extracting all the juice you can by pressing the berries. Return the juice to the pan with the sugar and boil gently for half an hour or so, stirring to make sure the sugar is dissolved. Pour through a funnel into warm, small sterilised plastic bottles, and screw the lids on tightly. Make in late summer or early autumn when the berries are ripe. It will be ready to use by Christmas.

PHOTOGRAPHY: LEE HICKMAN

Sweet fruit pickles

make in summer

After the elderflowers come the loquats, cherry plums, green walnuts, cherries, cornels, plums, greengages, mulberries, damsons, green hazelnuts, filberts, Turkish hazels, grapes and goji berries. My preserving came about as a way of utilising the stuff that either couldn't be eaten raw or was so abundant it seemed silly to waste. My cupboards soon began to fill with a varied selection of bottled and jarred delights, and I was able to enjoy sharing luxurious things that I could never ordinarily afford. Among my favourites are the loquats and mulberries, because you would never find them in the shops. I like the idea that they're sourced within a few minutes' bicycle ride from my house.

For local, seasonal tip-offs, and for recipes, links and advice on preserving, I set up a Facebook community page called Pickling Peckham – an Urban Forager's Guide. It details local availability as the season progresses; I also upload photographs and post updates about useful plants I've found. It's a good starting point for someone interested in the idea of putting truly local, seasonal produce to good use.

For those Peckhamites seeking safety in numbers, there's the Burgess Park Food Project Community Garden, and it's worthwhile checking for community food groups that may already be active in your area. There are also larger organisations like the London Orchard Project (*see p96*) and the London Abundance Network, which arrange the picking and distribution of fruit from local trees.

Pickling is a really easy way to preserve seasonal fruits. I love to pickle cherry plums, which appear in July. You'll see them covering the ground in parks, estates, schools – even by bus stops. About the size of a large cherry, the plums can be yellow, red or something in between.

Collecting them is a doddle, but teamwork is best – and the local street cleaners will be delighted. You'll need an old sheet and a very long stick. Whoever's tallest gets to shake the tree with the stick, and the others stand underneath dodging fruity missiles while trying to catch them in the sheet. Make sure to mind your head – a cycling helmet could come in handy.

This recipe for sweet fruit pickles works well with any kind of cherry (seasonal in July), or with wild plums, crab apples and damsons (August to September). Preserved in vinegar syrup, fruits can be spiced according to taste. They look good and are quick and easy to make. Small fruits are best pickled whole, so remind yourself of the stones when you label the jars.

Ingredients
* A dozen clusters of ripening, unblemished berries, or enough for the vinegar to just cover
* A litre of malt, cider or wine vinegar
* 275g of brown sugar
* Spices including cinnamon, allspice, peppercorns, mace, ginger, mustard seed, dried chilli

Method
For this you'll need fruit that's just coming up to ripe, and that's undamaged and unblemished; windfalls are probably no use, as they're likely to be bruised. The fruit should be carefully washed and completely dry before pickling can commence: wet fruit will dilute the vinegar and may affect the preserving quality. Sterilise some clean jam jars in an oven on a very low heat for ten minutes or so. Keep them warm, as you'll need to pot the pickles into hot jars. You'll need plastic-coated screw-top lids; recycled jars are fine. Boil the lids briefly to sterilise them, and then allow them to dry. Heat your vinegar with the spices. Add the sugar and stir. When the sugar has dissolved, gently lower in your fruit and bring to a simmer. Have your hot jars ready. When the fruit has slightly softened, but isn't mushy, remove it with a slotted spoon from the vinegar and pop it into the hot jars, making sure to keep the rims clean – any drips will affect the seal. Don't overfill the jars. Boil the remaining vinegar syrup for ten minutes or so, until it thickens to a syrupy consistency. Use it hot to fill the jars to within a quarter-inch of the top. Screw the lids on tightly and label.

Blackberry vinegar

In the early 1980s, riots were kicking off across Britain, and terrible housing, mass unemployment and inner-city decay made Peckham a tough place to be. In 2000 the authorities began the demolition of the Gloucester and North Peckham estates, where I'd been living. The schoolboy Damilola Taylor was murdered that year in our street, and the area was an ugly and frightening place to be. Heavily pregnant with my first child, I felt isolated and vulnerable.

As the area was redeveloped during the 2000s, the street was transformed and I was fortunate enough to be offered a home with a small garden. I planted a cherry tree and, as the surrounding estates were demolished, I rescued the best plants from nearby abandoned flats, taking cuttings and seeds and digging up the odd bulb.

Having been preoccupied with the ugliness of my surroundings, I wanted my youngsters to know that there were still beautiful things around them – I was and still am very concerned that thousands of children miss out on the natural world almost completely. My interest began in the garden, and soon moved out into all the open spaces around us.

During a period of hardship it was difficult to afford fresh fruit, and so I concentrated on the food that was available. We would pick blackberries and wild plums in the park, and apples and pears from a nearby abandoned garden. I tried to learn as much as I could about preserving, and identifying and using more unusual things.

It takes front to carry an 8-foot fruit-picking ladder through Peckham, but lots of people are interested in what you're doing and often stop to chat. Peckham has never been deficient in interesting characters, and you don't need to go up a tree to find one.

Most often I'm approached by ordinary passersby expressing an interest in what I'm doing. People are often surprised to discover there are so many things growing all around us. Women in burqas have stopped to help pick plums. An old Chinese lady stopped to tell me about the grapefruit tree I was admiring, and how its fragrant leaves are used ritually and medicinally in China and can be used

in the bath or stuffed into pillows. Homeless Polish gents chat with me in Burgess Park as we share the hazels from the native plantings, still green so as to beat the squirrels at their own game.

Families in the park pick blackberries together on the way home from school, and share recipes and tips on where to find the best berries. I love to take my children blackberrying: as they bicker over who has the best stick, and learn how to identify bugs, chase butterflies and make new friends, the adults put the world to rights. At leisure, conversation flows easily.

Delicious fresh or in puddings, blackberries also make great jams, jellies, pickles, chutneys, fruit leathers, syrups, wines, liqueurs and vinegars. A glove is useful for picking, and a damp cloth is essential for sticky hands. Making a fruit vinegar is a way to use up very ripe blackberries if you don't have time to make jelly or jam. It lasts all winter, and was traditionally used as a sore throat and cough remedy. It's also delicious as a dressing.

Ingredients
* 500g ripe blackberries
* 500ml good cider or malt vinegar
* Sugar (optional)

Method
Wash and drain your blackberries, and mash them up in a large plastic bowl. Add the vinegar, cover the bowl with a tea towel and leave for a few days while you hunt down, clean and sterilise suitable bottles with plastic lids or corks. Stir and mash the fruit each day. When the fruit is well macerated, strain it through clean muslin and measure the resulting juice into a stainless steel pan. For sweet vinegar syrup (good for drizzling and great for sore throats), add a pound of sugar per pint of liquid before bringing to the boil; you can leave the sugar out if you prefer. Boil the fruit vinegar for 10 minutes while skimming any scum from the surface. When it is completely clear, allow to cool before bottling.

A wassail cup

The stories that plants can tell are many and varied. Many of our common weeds and plants have traditional uses as remedies, dyes or household goods. Often they bear old legends and folklore that link us with the past and engage us with the natural world, acknowledging the seasons and the land to which we belong.

Yarrow is also known as "soldiers' woundwort", and was used to staunch the flow of blood on ancient battlefields. Rowan is a magical tree, sacred to many ancient cultures and used as protection against witches; its berries, combined with crab apples, can be used to make a beautiful rich ruby jelly. Ginkgo biloba is a common urban tree with known memory-enhancing properties and makes a revolting tincture or tea. Linden blossom, however, makes a fragrant tea that I can recommend as a safe and effective soother of the collywobbles in both adults and children.

In Peckham, to show our gratitude for last year's crops and our hopes for the coming season, we like to attempt a wassail – the old English tradition of singing to an orchard in the hope that it will provide a more abundant harvest. Awkwardly, we don't really have much wassailing experience between us, so after a bit of YouTubing we just make it up as we go along; there have been no arrests so far. It's probably just an excuse to get slightly inebriated, which you have to do to persuade yourself that singing to the trees in a public place is a good idea.

If you haven't got a convenient orchard to hand, it is perfectly acceptable to include any available fruit trees and foodie hedgerows in your plans. With sufficient wassail toasts, anything is possible. Invite your local samba band, learn some traditional wassailing songs and fashion some lanterns from jam jars and tea lights. Gird your loins with spicy mulled cider and roasted apples for the noisy amble through the park, and don't forget the toast. Alternatively, stay at home in the warm and invite your friends round for a traditional wassail cup and some rousing verse.

And the next time you pass your local fruit tree, don't forget to say thank you.

Old Apple tree, old apple tree
We've come to wassail thee
To bear and to bow apples enow
Hats full, caps full, three bushel bags full
Barn floors full and little heaps under the stairs!

Next crowne the bowle full
With gentle Lambs wooll
Adde sugar, nutmeg, and ginger
With store of ale too
And thus ye must doe
To make the Wassaile a swinger

Ingredients
* *Cooking apples or crab apples*
* *Brown sugar or honey to taste*
* *A stick or two of cinnamon*
* *A good pinch of nutmeg*
* *Several cloves*
* *Pinch of ground ginger*
* *A litre of apple juice*
* *A litre of good cider*
* *Some brandy (optional)*

Method
Roast your apples whole for 45 minutes or so in a hot oven, together with the spices and sugar and a splash of water. When they are cooked and soft, you can press them through a sieve into a large pan or just fish out the spices and chuck the apples into the pan whole. Add the apple juice and heat until simmering, turn down the heat and add the cider and a taste of honey if desired. Keep the mixture warm but don't let it come to the boil. Before serving add a splash of brandy should you wish to. "Lambswool" is the name given to the fluffy apple pulp that should float to the surface of the drink and add extra deliciousness.

Penny Greenhough can be found at
facebook.com/urbanforagerpeckhampickler

PHOTOGRAPHY: JOE MCGORTY

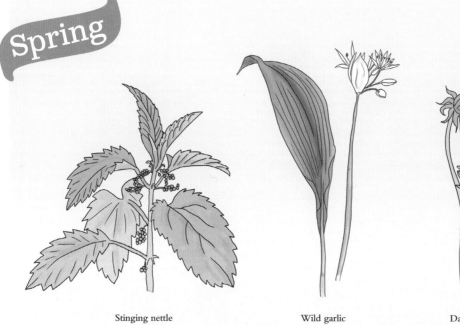

Stinging nettle   Wild garlic   Dandelion

Elderberry   Wild strawberry   Wild thyme

Blackberry

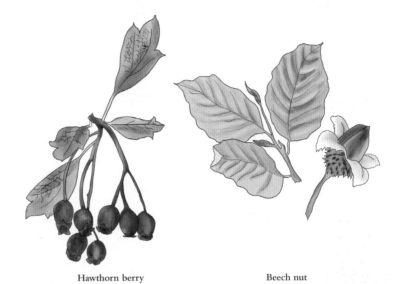

Hawthorn berry

Beech nut

Winter

Rowan

Cep

Rosehip

Small &
edible
gardening

RIZE

ETABLE

iA

You don't need a large garden to grow fruit and veg – a window sill or small balcony will do. In your own edible garden, you can grow food that is hard to buy, like alpine strawberries and edible flowers, as well as an amazing variety of produce that will adorn your plate and garden for months on end.

All crops need is a certain amount of light and shelter, some much more than others. The "sun-loving" need to be in the sun for about half the day in summer; and "shade-tolerant" plants prefer the sun, but will be fine in the shade.

Lighten dark corners with pale-painted walls, and protect windy sites with a trellis. Just make sure your roof, balcony or window sill is strong enough to support your containers, which will be heavy once filled with damp compost.

You can grow seeds or buy plants. Seeds are cheap and you have a greater choice, but they require space and care. Plants are a better choice if you only want one or two. Plugs are little plants that are usually available in groups of five – perfect for sharing between two tiny gardens. Buy them from a reputable supplier and plant them out as soon as you get them.

Finally, if you can, make room for a table and chairs. One of the great joys in life is eating a meal surrounded by the fresh flowers and produce you've grown.

Words by Jane McMorland Hunter
Photography by Patrick Dalton

Vegetables

Most vegetables are annuals: they go from seed to plate within a year, and often much less. Your containers will be constantly changing as you harvest crops and grow new ones; and if you move your pots around, your garden will always look amazing. Some plants, such as chard, can be harvested a few leaves at a time over a period of weeks, and "cut-and-come-again" lettuces will regrow three or four times. Most vegetables need a sunny spot, along with rich, well-drained soil and regular supplies of food and water. The minimum size of pot in which to grow most vegetables and flowers is 30cm (12in) across and deep. Use peat-free multi-purpose compost or vegetable compost.

Potatoes Earlies grow well in containers in full sun, and give you delicious little potatoes. Grow from specialist seed potatoes, planted in deep containers – at least 40cm (18in) – and add more compost as the plant grows to prevent the tubers from turning green. Water regularly and feed weekly as soon as the flowers appear. Do not plant near tomatoes as they may give each other blight – a horrible fungus that you'll want to avoid at all costs.

Tomatoes Tomatoes are technically fruits, but are grown (and eaten) as vegetables. Cherry tomatoes ripen easily outside in full sun and grow well in pots or troughs 30cm (12in) deep. Tumbling varieties can be grown in hanging baskets. Bushes can take up a lot of space, but cordons (single stems) climb neatly. Regular watering will prevent the fruits from splitting and a weekly feed will ensure a good crop. Keep away from potatoes.
For more on growing tomatoes in the city, see p106

Peas and beans Mangetout and sugar snap peas and dwarf French, runner and broad beans have pretty flowers, and crop well in containers with a minimum depth of 30cm (12in). Provide support for them to climb and harvest regularly when the pods are small. Borlotti beans should be left until the beans have swollen in the pod. They will all tolerate a little shade, but crop better in full sun.

Sweetcorn This needs a long hot summer, regular water and a sheltered spot, but the rewards are great in both looks and taste. They are wind-pollinated and need to be planted in a block; a double row in a window box looks amazing.

Squash and courgettes Halloween pumpkins will take over your garden, but patty pan squash (the flying saucers), little pumpkins and courgettes can be trained to climb rather than trail. The container should be at least 45cm (18in) deep and filled with rich compost. Position in full sun, give them plenty of water and feed fortnightly. One of the joys of growing courgettes is that you can eat the flowers, which are totally delicious stuffed, dipped in batter and fried. Use the male flowers (the ones with a narrow stalk rather than a baby courgette at the base) and you won't even reduce your harvest.

Radishes These are quick and easy to grow, and invaluable for filling in gaps. You can sow seeds and a month later you will have a crop of pink, white, yellow or even purple radishes. They will grow in shallow containers and are happy in a bit of shade, but they do need to be watered regularly or their roots will turn woody.

Leaves Rocket, spinach, chard, lettuce and oriental greens will all grow happily in containers and give you long harvests. Rainbow chard has brightly coloured stems, rocket has pretty, edible flowers and lettuce leaves can be red, green or purple, ruffled, crimped or floppy. Most will grow in shallow containers and prefer a little shade. Just don't let them dry out or they will bolt and run to seed.

Other vegetables to grow in the sun
Chilli peppers, aubergines, onions and cucumbers.

And those that will tolerate a little shade
Carrots, beetroot, rhubarb and kale.

Which container

You can use any container that will hold soil and allow water to drain through. Big pots will make a small space seem larger, and are better for plants. Tiny pots tend to dry out and are really only suitable for small herbs. A long trough is more attractive than a grow bag and better for the plants, as it is deeper and gives their roots more room. Hanging baskets are perfect for tumbling tomatoes, strawberries and herbs, but you may need to water them twice a day in warm weather. Always put broken crocks in the bottom of the pot to ensure good drainage, and use potting compost; ordinary garden soil will not support plants in containers.

Potatoes
Grow well in containers in full sun

Harvest new potatoes and pair with smoked mackerel, see p168

Little pumpkins
Opt for these varieties in small spaces

Runner beans
Produce lovely flowers and crop well in containers

Cherry tomatoes
Grow tumbling varieties in hanging baskets

Delicious as a savoury tatin, see p170

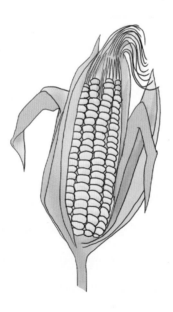

Sweetcorn
Need long, hot summers but look great in window boxes

Radishes
Low-maintenance, quick-growing and colourful crops

Fruit

Fruits are divided into two categories: top, such as apples and pears, which are grown on trees; and soft, such as berries and currants, which are grown on bushes or canes. Many will thrive in containers. Fruit requires pollination, which means you either need to grow more than one type or choose a self-fertile variety. Most need shelter from strong winds and a certain amount of sunshine. You will probably have to share some of your harvest with the birds, but birds are a bonus in a garden too. Every spring you should mulch round the plants with garden compost or well-rotted manure. You should also feed them fortnightly during summer, and ensure that the soil remains moist but not soggy throughout the year.

Fruit will need a pot at least 45cm (18in) across and deep, and should be grown in specialist compost such as John Innes No 3. As fruits are long-lived plants, choose disease-resistant varieties and always buy them from a reputable nursery.

Strawberries Alpine and wild strawberries are easy to grow and produce a luscious and almost unbuyable crop. They are happy in semi-shade, produce tiny fruits throughout the summer and tend to be ignored by birds. They have shallow roots and can be grown as decorative edging or in hanging baskets. Terracotta "strawberry pots" are not ideal, as they rarely enable the lower plants to get enough water.

Blackberries The fruit grow on long stems, but these can easily be trained into beautiful twisting patterns along a wall or trellis; thornless varieties make this much easier. They will grow in the shade, but taste sweeter if they've been out in the sun. After the harvest, cut back the stems that have fruited and train the new shoots into place for the following year.

Blueberries These are nicely shaped bushes with pretty cream flowers, delicious berries and a beautiful autumn colour. They need acidic soil, so plant them in ericaceous compost and ideally keep them moist with rainwater. They fruit best if you have two different varieties and position them in full sun.

Figs These are perfect for containers, because if their roots are restricted they produce more fruit. They need to be grown against a warm sheltered wall, as the baby fruits grow throughout the winter. Trim the long stems back in spring to encourage the plant to produce fruits rather than leaves.

Gooseberries Difficult to buy, yet easy to grow, gooseberries are perfect container plants. They are fine in semi-shade, and enjoy moist soil and an airy position. They are grown most commonly as bushes, but you can also grow a cordon, train them in a fan against a wall or grow a half-standard (lollipop). Dessert varieties can be eaten straight from the bush.

Fruit trees Most fruit trees are grafted on to a rootstock, which means that, within reason, you can have the type of fruit you want on a size of tree you can accommodate in your garden. Trees can be trained as cordons, fans, espaliers and candelabras if space is tight. Ready-trained trees are expensive but worth the money, as the formative pruning is done for you. Apples, pears, quinces, cherries and plums are all hardy, whereas peaches and citrus are more delicate.

Grapes These need full sun, a large, deep container and strong supports to climb.
For more on growing grapes in the city, see p76

Raspberries These fruits will tolerate some shade but are unattractive plants, so only grow them if you really love the fruit.

Rhubarb This is technically a vegetable – with the same logic that makes tomato a fruit. Some varieties are compact and will grow in sun or semi-shade.

Currants These do best in sunshine and need an airy, yet sheltered site. They also require large pots, at least 60cm (2ft) deep.

Container care

Looking after containers is easy but must be done regularly. You will need to water them every day or two – probably even if it rains – and feed them once a week. You can add water-retaining gels to the compost but you will still need to water it. Use liquid seaweed for general growth and tomato food to encourage flowers and fruits to mature. Adding a mulch (garden or mushroom compost, or composted bark) will retain water and benefit the plants: always leave a gap round the plant so the stem doesn't rot.

Strawberries
Grow varieties you can't buy like
Alpine and wild strawberries

Gooseberries
Perfect container plants that enjoy
most soil and semi-shade

Blueberries
Fruit best if you have two
different varieties

*Harvest when the fruits turn
deep blue and turn into seasonal
scones, see p172*

Figs
Love containers and a warm
sheltered wall

Blackberries
Look beautiful growing
along a wall or trellis

*Harvest in autumn and make
into blackberry vinegar, see p134*

Pears
Hardy trees that can be grown
against a wall or trellis

Herbs and edible flowers

It is easy to be self-sufficient in delicious, fresh herbs, even in a tiny space. They are compact plants and love growing in containers – and when it comes to cooking, a little goes a long way. Many come from the Mediterranean: they like hot, dry conditions, and taste stronger when grown in the sun. A combination of cold and damp will kill them. Add grit to their compost, do not feed them, and water them early in the day so they do not go to bed with wet feet. A smaller group (see below) will tolerate some shade, and like moister, richer soil.

Woody herbs, such as rosemary, sage and bay, will last many years and should be grown in a pot at least 20cm (8in) wide and deep. Allow them to dry out a bit in winter, and protect bay from frost as it has shallow roots. Mint and chives have deep roots and like to be grown in similar-sized pots, but all other herbs can be grown in small pots or clumped together in a window box. Do not grow two different varieties of the same herb together, such as peppermint and apple mint, as this will reduce the flavour. Mint should be grown in a pot on its own; it spreads by growing runners, and will take over your garden given half a chance.

Many herbs are annuals or short-lived perennials, and are best replaced each year. You can grow them from seed or buy little plants. Basil, chervil, coriander, dill and sorrel grow easily from seed. Supermarket plants should be split up and repotted – they are grown for looks rather than longevity and too many seedlings are usually crammed into a small pot.

Herbs for the sun
Basil, bay, chamomile, coriander, dill, fennel, French tarragon, garlic, lavender, oregano, rosemary, sage, savory, sweet marjoram and thyme.

Herbs that like a little shade
Chervil, chives, mint, parsley and sorrel.

Slugs and snails

Slugs and snails are the worst pests: put copper tape round the rim of pots and sprinkle fine grit round each plant to deter them. And don't be tempted to spray your plants with chemicals: make sure they have good growing conditions and they will be able to withstand most pests and diseases.

Flowers can bring colour and fragrance to a garden, and will improve your crops by encouraging pollinating insects. Many can also be used in the kitchen to bring colour and flavour to your cooking.

Depending on the flower, you can sprinkle them on salads, vegetables and puddings, cook them in cakes and biscuits, mix them in oil, vinegar, sugar or butter, crystallise them for use as cake decorations, or serve them in drinks. Always check which parts of the plant are edible – potato flowers are very pretty but poisonous. All these flowers will produce more blooms if grown in the full sun.

Borage (*Borago officinalis*)
This grows in attractive clumps, which are covered with dainty star-shaped flowers in blue, white and occasionally pink. The flowers look lovely scattered on salads and vegetables, and can be frozen in ice trays to make beautiful and unusual ice cubes.

Nasturtiums (*Tropaeolum*)
The entire plant is edible – flowers, leaves and seeds. It tastes peppery and will add flavour as well as colour to a dish. Nasturtiums grow best in full sun and very poor soil – you could use dust sweepings and they would still flourish. Grow climbing or trailing varieties and let them run riot.

Violas (*Viola*)
These are invaluable, as they flower in winter and early spring when most other flowers have shut down. They can be sprinkled on salads and soups or crystallised on cakes and chocolate. The tricoloured heartsease is the daintiest.

Edible flowers on herbs and vegetables
Chives, coriander, courgettes, lavender, radishes, rocket, rosemary and thyme.

Ornamental edible flowers
Anchusa, daisies, hollyhocks, pinks, pot marigolds, primroses, roses, salvias, scented geraniums and sunflowers.

Sweet peas
These aren't edible, but every kitchen garden needs them. They climb neatly, flower for months on end, smell wonderful and will provide you with continuous posies for the kitchen table.

Mint
Can be grown on a window sill.
Likes partial shade

Lavender
Great for bees. Basks in a sunny
spot and well-drained soil

Nasturtium
Easy to look after and totally
edible; flowers, seeds and all

Viola
Brings colour to your garden in
winter and early spring

Rosemary
Likes full sun and shelter.
Easy to propagate from cuttings

*Mix into a marinade for
a gorgeous confit duck, see p182*

Basil
Thrives in a sunny spot, but not
direct sunlight. Can be grown
indoors during winter

City
chicks

From her home in Brentford, Sara Ward has been staging a quiet revolution against packaged food, aided and abetted by an enthusiastic team of chickens.

Hen Corner is a garden packed with beehives, fruit trees and a closely guarded vegetable patch. Culinary feasts, ranging from homemade cider to hollandaise sauce, are produced within its walls. Unsurprisingly, eggs take centre stage in much of the cooking, and entire meals can be made without having to open a single box, jar or tin.

Sara's chicken coops might seem too ambitious for a novice keeper, but Hen Corner has not always been so productive. The Ward family's dream of self-sufficiency started with just two birds and a potato plant growing in a dustbin. A few hundred eggs later and Sara has shown that, with a bit of earth and enough imagination, anyone can keep poultry.

To help give you a feel for what it might be like to have birds of your own, here is a glimpse into Sara's day-to-day life.

As Hen Corner meanders gently through the seasons, it is clear that hens never allow city life to become ordinary or grey. In fact, fresh eggs come in colours – blue, green or speckled brown – that supermarkets can only dream of. It is a whole world of choice that is not restricted by what you can find on a shelf. And if you try it, just like Sara, you may never look back.

Words by Camila Ruz
Photography by Adam Johann Lang

Chicken diary

Spring: egg hunt

My first two chickens were called Pepsi and Shirley, named after the backing singers from Wham. We lived in a small terraced house with a garden just 8 metres by 10. I had never touched so much as a budgie before then but, there I was, with a present of two fluffy hens and a plastic hut.

After a few days of stroking and handling the chickens, I took a trip to the supermarket. Wandering down the meat aisle, I picked up an oven-ready bird and felt the same body shape as that of my own hens. When we eat chicken, we all know what animal it comes from, but it was a sudden shock to connect the bird on the shelf to the one flapping around in my garden.

Questioning where our food came from was what led my family to get chickens in the first place. At the time, people were only just beginning to look into organic foods and the impact of pesticides. I started to do a little research of my own and found that once you know, you cannot unknow.

In those years, the demand for milk as a basic item and the monopoly of the big supermarkets had led to hundreds of British dairy farmers going out of business. It made me cross with the food production giants. I thought, "all I want to do is to grow enough food to make a whole meal from my own garden, just one meal."

I started to grow all sorts of things: courgettes, apple trees, even potatoes in a dustbin. My search for a home-grown meal led to the question of fresh eggs. Pepsi laid the first. Nature lets chickens break in gently. Pure-breed birds will not start laying until they are 18-to-20 weeks old. Their first egg usually coincides with Valentine's Day, whereas hybrid chickens start to lay much earlier. In both types, the eggs are small to start off with, and only gradually get bigger.

This egg was particularly small but, undeterred, I boiled it lightly and served it with smoked salmon.

A move to Brentford and a bigger garden allowed us

Choose a breed

Pure breeds such as the Rhode Island Red are more expensive, but keeping them can help to preserve a heritage breed. Always buy from a reputable breeder and ensure the birds conform to the British Poultry Standards. Hybrids are much cheaper and are often recommended for beginners because they can be more resistant to disease. Remember that all breeds vary in temperament, so it is important to research which conditions a particular breed requires to thrive.

Buy chickens at an age of around four to five months when they are just starting to lay eggs and are easy to look after.

Brahma
Egg colour: Tinted
Productivity 150 eggs a year
Type: Heavy
Behaviour: Mostly gentle, happy to be handled
Urban suitability: Good

Andalusian
Egg colour: White
Productivity: 200 eggs a year
Type: Light
Behaviour: Semi-adaptable to confinement but prefers free range; active, flighty, noisy
Urban suitability: So-so

Dorking
Egg colour: White
Productivity: 190 eggs a year
Type: Heavy
Behaviour: Stately & awkward; fattens easily; happy to be handled
Urban suitability: So-so

to go from two chickens to nine. As spring is the peak of the egg season, we usually have enough to spare for an Easter egg party. The children hunt for chocolate eggs among the shrubbery and then decorate the real ones in the kitchen.

Our children are involved in a lot of what we do, and the entire family waits anxiously for our new chicks to hatch in late May. It was only last year that we did it for the first time. This spring, we bought a pack of six fertilised Orpington chicken eggs off eBay for £8, including postage and packaging.

I usually like having a mix of breeds and a variety of coloured eggs, from pale blue to a creamy white, but the Orpington bird is so irresistible in its temperament. Whether it is a Buff Orpington, such as Butternut, or a chocolate-brown bantam such as Ascot, the breed really is quite soppy. You can pick one up and have a cup of tea with it sitting on your lap.

Plymouth Rock
Egg colour: **Tinted**
Productivity: **200 eggs a year**
Type: **Heavy**
Behaviour: **Calm & docile; sociable in a mixed flock**
Urban suitability: **Good**

Welsummer
Egg colour: **Dark red-brown**
Productivity: **200 eggs a year**
Type: **Heavy**
Behaviour: **Lively but more docile than flighty**
Urban suitability: **Good**

Summer: feathering the nest

We run our chicken-keeping courses from May through to September. People come straight from their offices in the city and spend an evening learning how to handle hens and muck out coops. It is important to try to imagine what it would be like to have a chicken in your garden before getting your own, so a little hands-on experience is a great way to ease yourself in.

Our pupils are always surprised at how low-maintenance our chickens are. But then again, I do not have all that much time for intensive animal keeping, either. I work part-time, my husband works full-time and we are responsible for a young family, as well has having active roles in our community. It might be a Hen Corner day today, but tomorrow is always just another day in the office.

The basic to-do list for looking after chickens consists of feeding, watering and collecting the eggs regularly. You only need to empty the droppings tray into the compost once a week, and all the tasks are quick enough to fit into almost any routine to keep precious weekends free.

Chickens require a little more care when they are ill. The hens can be more prone to mites in summer and, since establishing that London vets are not all that clued up when it comes to chickens, I tend to treat them at home. Prevention really is better than the cure, and with clean coops, dirt for dust baths and, of course, a good diet, keeping your chickens healthy should not prove too difficult. A couple of times a year, the houses also need a good strip down and scrub. It is one of those jobs I usually try to bribe the kids to do.

Since both my children are still at school, we always have the sacrosanct event of the summer holiday. Whether it is to deep France or the West Country, we always take an empty pet carrier with us. There have been countless opportunities missed because we had no way to carry a chicken home from holiday. You can find all kinds of unusual poultry breeds at village fairs, so now we always throw the carrier in the back of the car, just in case.

People often think that keeping animals means becoming chained to your chicken coop, but we have never found it difficult to find people to look after our birds. The bees can be more of an issue. A neighbour's colony was expanding last year, so we made the most of it and acquired a hive. There are times when you need to don the white suit and marigolds weekly, so we try and time our holidays around the bee inspections. But going away when you have chickens has never been a problem, and our chicken sitters always go home well rewarded in eggs. Having said that, it is best not to assume that everyone will know to take the eggs home with them every day. On one memorable occasion, I forgot to be specific and came home to find each hen staggering up an egg mountain. I had to take a saucepan outside to collect them all.

How to recognise a healthy bird

Comb
Beak
Wattle
Ear
Sickles
Hackles
Breast
Body feathers
Hock
Toe
Spur

Right: Rev Steve Paynter from St Mary's in Ealing keeps a flock of hens, new chicks and two Gloucester Old Spots pigs. Below: Dave Griffin, an accountant in the City, has two chickens called Virginia and Harriet. Below, right: Actress Esther Coles and her husband keep their chickens on an allotment in Crouch End.

1 *Does the bird have dry combs and wattles?* There should be no leaking fluids

2 *Are the beaks, nostrils and vent feathers clean?* No leaking fluids, the eyes should be clean and bright with equal-sized pupils and the vents should not have a bad smell

3 *Are the toes straight and the leg scales smooth?* Upward-lifting scales can be a sign of scaly leg mite

4 *Are there any bald patches?* Dull and disordered feathers can mean illness or stress

5 *Does the chicken seem alert and active?* Regular handling is the only way to tell if a chicken has lost weight

Autumn: an apple a day

September is the time for cider. We are lucky enough to have two apple trees in our garden. It may seem difficult to believe, with the nearby grey tower blocks filling up the sky, but the whole area used to be orchard land and our 150-year-old trees are, in fact, older than the house. There are actually plenty of people in London who know of an apple tree with an overabundance of fruits and every year we invite our friends and neighbours to bring their spare apples along to Cider Sunday.

Sending the children up the trees to gather the fruit, we adults keep ourselves busy by splitting into production teams. Together we spend a sticky afternoon washing, chopping, crushing and pressing. Once everyone is covered head to toe with apple residue, we fill up the sterilised demijohns and shut the airlocks. The natural yeasts in the air and on the apples ferment the juice for us. Since the whole cider-making is an experiment, we sometimes vary the recipe and try a second ferment, adding a little sugar to an airtight lemonade bottle. The gases that are released will help produce a slightly sweeter, sparkling cider that is ready for drinking by Christmas.

Events such as Cider Sunday give us an excuse to share our harvests with our friends. This is especially fun now that we have a small vegetable patch under the kitchen window. Apart from our eggs, my favourite produce is the asparagus. Think for a minute about how old a bunch of asparagus might be in a shop – a few days? A week? Now imagine what it tastes like when it is eaten within minutes of being snapped straight out from the ground.

Humans are not the only animals that find my vegetables tasty. I have to regularly defend my kitchen garden from marauding chickens. All the seedlings, from broad beans to brassica, need a vigilant eye, as some hens have a real talent for escaping. We have one bird who is Houdini-like in her abilities. As a youngster, she learned that she could take a flying leap from the top of her hut on to my lawn. From there, it is only a hop, skip and a jump into my lettuce. Whenever I spot her, I race into the garden and start clapping. This may sound ridiculous, but chickens that have been handled regularly from an egg seem much easier to catch and manage. Like a trained soldier, she stops at the signal and walks herself back into her run, trailing my pea seedlings behind her.

What the chickens do not plunder we can use during our Harvest Fair Trade. The strap line is make it, bake it, grow it and sow it. The idea is to trade items that people have made themselves. No money is necessary. I normally take along boxes of fresh eggs and some of my elderflower liqueur. It gives us a real sense of community to see other people making their own produce and to spend some time swapping tips and appreciating each other's skill. You never stop learning. Along with the regular profusion of jams, cakes and chutneys, we also get more unusual items. Last year a man dropped by with a sack of firewood.

Winter: Sunday roast

Chickens are hardy creatures as long as you keep them warm and dry. When food becomes scarce, the London fox is more of a challenge in winter than the cold. The first of our chickens we ever ate was the victim of a day-time fox attack.

It was Christmas and bitterly cold. I was in the shower when movement caught my eye from the window. I turned to see a fox on the lawn with a hen in its mouth. Running out into the snow in my dressing gown I shouted at the top of my lungs, wet hair flying all over the place. Miraculously, we managed to save Cuckoo and she survived with only a few teeth marks on her back to show for it. Another chicken was not so lucky. We found her lying dead in the frosty grass.

She had been such a healthy bird that it seemed a shame to throw the carcass away. I had read plenty of articles on how to butcher a chicken but I had never attempted to do it in real life. My husband was not convinced. He was worried about the diseases the fox might have been carrying. We compromised and I discarded anything that had been near the fox's mouth and jointed the rest for dinner.

We only intended to have our chickens for their eggs, but since then we have kept three males for meat. Having cockerels in London is not a good way of endearing yourself to your neighbours, so we only keep them until they start to call out at ungodly hours of the morning.

It is difficult to describe how loud male chickens can be. The noise has a habit of carrying across the walls of their plastic huts and piercing you right through the double glazing.

We chose to use the plastic Eglu huts rather than the wooden variety because they are completely fox-proof when locked for the night. Day-time visits can still be a problem, but once dusk arrives, you can usually sleep easy. That is as long as you have counted the inhabitants properly. A few years ago I made the fatal mistake of failing to see a hen roosting in my vegetable patch and, by the morning, she was gone. I now meticulously count my chickens every night. The plastic huts are also easier to keep clean. The challenge with the wooden houses is that there are plenty of nooks and crannies for red mite to hide inside, whereas the Eglu comes apart like a Lego model. The money we spent on buying a hutch rather than building our own was money we have saved on eggs over the years.

I doubt our hens will ever earn us lots of money, but they bring their own rewards and have become part of our day-to-day life. We still sometimes toy with the idea of moving to the countryside but, here in London, we already have everything we need. Whenever I hear my hens clucking triumphantly over their eggs or I manage to salvage some brassicas from the garden, I see living proof that you can grab handfuls of country earth, stuff them into the cement of your everyday life and watch things grow.

Handling your chickens

The more you handle your birds, the easier it is to catch them when you need to. Chickens should be handled gently, but supportively. Rest its weight on your left forearm with its head under your arm. The legs should be between the fingers of your left hand and its "dangerous end" should be pointing away from you.

Moving houses can be quite stressful for chickens so they will need a week before they understand that the hut is their home. Some birds might also need a little encouragement to get up any ladders into their hut for the first time.

House your hens

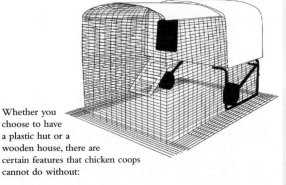

Whether you choose to have a plastic hut or a wooden house, there are certain features that chicken coops cannot do without:

1 At least 2.5 metres of floor space for each bird
2 Perches for the birds to stand on while they sleep
3 Exercise space or a run outdoors
4 Dirt in the outside run for the chickens to scratch and take dust baths in. This will help hens to avoid mite infestations in the summer
5 A nesting box with wood shavings for the hens to lay her eggs in

Beekeeping

Whether you have a large garden, a tiny roof terrace, or no outside space at all, any Londoner can get involved with beekeeping and reap the rewards of this fascinating hobby.

Community hives in parks and on rooftops mean you can learn alongside others and share the workload. Simon Wilks and Amy Lee are two Londoners who are working with bees in this way. Here they tell their stories of urban beekeeping, and about working with these creatures for wider social aims.

Simon is the guardian of the London Beekeeping Association hives at Brockwell Park Community Greenhouses Apiary, and has two hives of his own in a friend's garden. Amy co-founded The Honey Club, a social enterprise that began on the empty rooftop of her office in King's Cross.

You might expect bees to be more suited to rural areas, but they thrive in London.

A diversity of flowering plants in our parks and gardens means urban honey has around 22 kinds of pollen, reflecting the variety of native and exotic plants in our city.

But it isn't all about the honeybee. There are 267 other wild varieties of solitary bees and bumblebees in the UK, which are all important pollinators, and which also need our help.

Leave a pile of dead leaves in your garden for bumblebees to nest in, grow bee-friendly flowering plants on your window sill, or just fix a "bee hotel" box to a south-facing outside wall – we can all help London's bees to flourish.

Words by Simon Wilks. Edited by Ellie Tennant, p156. Words by Amy Lee, p160

Spring: swarming warning

As buds burst forth to leaf and flower and sunshine tempts the idle into parks and gardens, the beekeeper is busy – anxiously peeping into his hives – for April heralds the arrival on nature's stage of the errant bugbear: swarming.

From now until the end of June, honeybees are inclined to swarm. This is perfectly natural and it is expected of them. If they did not swarm, they would never start new colonies, and honeybees would have gone the way of the Great Auk.

For the beekeeper, it is annoying. It means losing half the bees in a colony, and much of the productivity of a hive, so swarms are to be avoided at all costs.

In the countryside, a swarm does not matter much, but, in London they are often more obvious. Ten thousand bees standing still would not take up more space than a toaster, but bees can cover a lot of sky when you're standing under them, and they buzz a lot. Towns and cities contain lots of places that bees can live in, most of which aren't trees. Chimneys and roof-spaces, for example, make tempting homes for honeybees.

Controlling swarming is a tricky business, and it requires constant vigilance. Each hive must be inspected every week to check whether the bees are up to anything and, if they are, to do something about it. Even then, we may miss something, and the bees might swarm anyway, which is when we will get a phone call about our bees being a nuisance and then we have to leave work to try to catch them or,

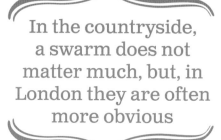

> In the countryside, a swarm does not matter much, but, in London they are often more obvious

just as often, watch them disappear over the rooftops.

Happily, there are some things we can do that seem to reduce the urge to swarm. Keep the bees busy by refurbishing their home with fresh, clean frames for them to build wax in. It will only work for a while, but as old wax comb can harbour bee diseases, it is a good idea to change all the frames every year or two in any case.

There are two ways of changing the frames in a hive. One is to prepare a whole new box of clean frames and to shake the bees out of the old box into the new, then destroy the old frames. This is very hygienic, but it does mean getting rid of all the baby bees, which is not nice. We sometimes use this method, but usually only when the hive is obviously suffering from a serious disease.

The second way, known as the "Bailey Method", involves putting a new set of frames above the existing one and, when new wax combs have been built and the queen is laying eggs in them, putting in a barrier to stop her going back to the old frames. Then, when all the larvae have emerged from the old frames, the whole bottom set can be removed and cleaned or disposed of.

We have now started this on one of our hives and it's not going to plan. After a week, the bees have managed to completely ignore the new box. However, since they're not showing any signs of swarming, it won't matter too much if they take their time.

Know your bees

Spring is the time for...

finding new queens. Look carefully and regularly for queen cells, which will be found hanging from the comb. If you see any, find the existing queen, put her with a new brood box filled with wax foundation and put the box on the site of the original hive. Place the other bees with the new queen cells somewhere else and they'll raise a new queen. All the flying bees will return to the existing queen, fooled into thinking that there has already been a swarm. Dividing the colony in this way prevents swarming.

Drone   Queen   Worker

Purifying wax

Summer is the time for...

purifying wax. Put rainwater (which is naturally soft) in the bottom of an old vegetable steamer. Place the impure wax that you've sliced off from the combs to access the honey in the vegetable basket, then heat slowly until it simmers. The wax will melt and drip through the holes, then float on the water. When the water cools down, you'll be left with a cake of wax on the surface with all the impurities at the bottom, which you can slice off carefully with a warm knife. Use the wax to make candles or furniture polish, or trade it in to a beekeeping supplies company for making wax foundation.

Gustavo Montes de Oca, 31, Bethnal Green
"I first started beekeeping in Afghanistan, working with refugees. Now, I work with The Golden Company, using beekeeping to give people business and life skills. Well-being, problem-solving, sustainability, organising, co-operation and collaboration — bees are a medium through which people can learn a lot. We have four colonies in St Mary's Secret Garden, Hackney, and the honey is a real melange of flavours, thanks to the diverse mix of local flowers. When you first cut off the wax caps, the honey flavour is the strongest, then it gradually fades every day. Bees have a rhythm that is undecipherable to us, but completely natural — it echoes something about the way the world is. I always lose track of time when I'm with the bees."

Summer: nectar points

It's happening. The lime trees and brambles are in flower, and our honeybees are all over them collecting nectar. At this time of year, when days are long, honeybee colonies are at their fullest and strongest. The amount of nectar available depends on the right balance of rain and sunshine, and on how well plants have done earlier in the year — but, if it is there, the bees will get it.

As well as bringing nectar home, the bees have got to squeeze the water out of it. They can do that all by themselves but, because watery nectar takes up more space than honey does, they need lots of room, preferably in wax combs they've already made. A careful beekeeper will have been stacking honey boxes (or "supers") on the hives since April, adding new ones when necessary so there's plenty of space for drying nectar in.

In June, during the main swarming season, we put one of the swarms in a little box called a nucleus hive. We had an empty hive knocking about, so we're populating it with the bees. That is trickier than it might seem. We are moving the bees to a different position within the apiary, so we cannot just move the frames from one hive to another without half of them flying straight back to where they used to live.

To prevent this, we have to move them when most of the flying bees are in the hive (either late in the evening or early in the morning) and lock them in for a few days, while they forget their way home. We give them some thin sugar syrup as a nectar substitute and, thanks to a mesh floor in the new hive, they don't suffocate, either.

By the autumn, they'll have built up into a full-size colony and, with any luck, the new colony will survive the winter.

We are also busy preparing an observation hive and cutting honeycomb to sell at the Lambeth Country Show in September at Brockwell Park. This involves a sharp knife, a steady hand and a cake rack so the slices of comb can drain nicely, without getting everything sticky. You also need gloves, a hat and — if necessary — a beard-guard, together with clean hands and a basic knowledge of food hygiene. Then, you just need some boxes to put the slices in, and some labels.

To prepare for harvest, we need to separate the bees from the honey, which is done by putting a little gate between the honey boxes we intend to harvest, and the rest of the hive. The bees can only go one way through the gate, and, within a couple of days, the honey boxes should have no bees in them. We've been harvesting liquid honey rather than cut-comb, and that involves a lot of equipment and somebody's kitchen. It's a sticky task and, to stand a chance, you've got to target people who've never extracted honey before.

When the honey is "ripe" (the bees have evaporated most of the water out of it), the bees cover each cell with a thin layer of white wax. To get the honey out, the first step — and the stickiest — is to remove that layer with an uncapping knife. We catch the wax, and a fair amount of honey, in a bucket.

Autumn: sticky situation

September is the month when all the local end-of-summer shows and events seem to happen, including the Thames Festival, the Bromley and Orpington Honey Show and, closer to home, a series of cookery demonstrations, plant sales and workshops at our Brockwell Community Greenhouses.

It's been nearly two months since we harvested the honey; it's been sitting in buckets to let bubbles of air and fragments of wax rise to the surface. This takes a while, because honey is sticky.

Bottling honey sounds simple. You hold the jar under the bucket, open the gate for a bit, close the gate and put a lid on the jar. This assumes your bucket has a honey gate at the bottom, which is less of a tap and more of a hole with a cover, designed on the assumption that an ordinary tap or spigot would get gummed up quickly, and be difficult to clean.

It also assumes you have remembered to loosen the airtight lid on the bucket. If you forget, you will suffer from glooping, which is messy. Not that it is not messy anyway; once honey is on your fingers, even if you're wearing gloves, it gets on the jars and the lids, on the scales and the floor and the table!

You might wonder – given all the regulations about weights and measures – how small-scale beekeepers are supposed to get their honey in jars without using a state-of-the-art bottling plant. The answer is that we buy jars of the right size and fill them up. Ideally, bottling should be done on a warm, dry evening, when the wasps are asleep and the honey flows quickly. Happily, the honey's already been through a double-sieve at extraction, so it's reasonably clear. You can strain the honey through a very fine mesh after that, which makes it as clear and bright as a pint of beer. But many customers want a "whole" product, and prefer their honey to have a bit of "haze" to it, caused by tiny particles, such as pollen grains. Another cause of "haze" is the formation of tiny sugar crystals. All honey will crystallize over time, and there's no easy way to tell how long it will take unless it's all been made from one type of nectar.

Usually the process takes a few months, but it can be delayed for a long time by heat-treating the honey, which dissolves the crystals and makes it clearer. This seems to be a selling point in supermarket honey, but our customers, thankfully, prefer their honey untreated.

We now have 48 jars of honey, which we'll sell nearer Christmas. That means our total harvest is 49lb of honey. The real harvest will have been a bit more than that, but spillages and inefficiency can mount up impressively. The bees themselves have collected much more than that, but they will have eaten some of it, and we let each hive keep around 20lb of honey. A hive needs around 40lb of stores to get through the winter, and although they may be able to collect that in August and September, and we can feed them with sugar syrup if they do not, it is both unwise and pretty mean to steal all of it.

> **Ideally, bottling should be done on a warm, dry evening, when the wasps are asleep**

How to guard against pests

Varroa mite

House mouse

Autumn is the time for...

treating bees for varroa – parasitic mites that live in all hives and can kill colonies if left to thrive. The idea is to kill mites before the harsh winter months so that the bees are as varroa-free as possible before the cold weather sets in, and therefore stand a better chance of survival. You don't want to risk contaminating honey, so this is the best time to treat them, after the harvest. Another pest to tackle is mice – they like to nest in warm beehives and can damage the comb, so mouse-guard grills should be fitted at hive entrances before the weather gets colder.

The London Honey Festival celebrates local honey

Keep an eye on your hive

Winter is the time for...

making regular (weekly) checks to ensure that all is well. In high winds, it is common for hives to blow over – especially those that are on rooftops or in exposed spots. Weight them down well with bricks or pieces of concrete. You've safe-guarded against mice, but also be aware of hungry woodpeckers, who like to attack beehives in the winter months, pecking holes in the wood and eating the bees as they come out. They can do a lot of damage in a short time and prevention is always better than cure, so make a rough cover from chicken wire mesh to stop them landing on the hives.

Tom Moggach, 36, Chalk Farm

"I keep bees in Kentish Town City Farm – I've had them for three years. Once you've found a good site for your bees, you're away! I get a sense of overwhelming fascination – you always learn from bees. There's a wonderful sense of peace that comes from watching a hive at work. I love the light-coloured, summer honey – it's floral and fragrant – a distillation of the diverse flowers in this area. I get darker, ivy honey later in the year, too."

PHOTOGRAPHY: STEPHANIE WOLFF

Winter: hives of inactivity

Snow is forecast, and we have placed a block of candy (baker's fondant) over the hole in the crown board, which sits on the top of the hive under the roof and has a hole in it for bees to feed through.

Fondant is not, perhaps, the best food for bees, but it is a close second. It is a mixture of glucose and sucrose and water, which are the main ingredients of nectar, though the proportions are very different. Why do we need to feed them? After all, the bees have had three whole months to make up the difference, and there's been no shortage of ivy or fuchsias for them to forage on. In fact, in September, all the hives were nice and heavy with new honey that had been stored for winter. Since July, the number of bees in each hive has been falling, too, and the queen has been laying fewer eggs. So there is less demand for honey, and more room to store it around the brood nest, and gradually the hives get heavier.

There are two things to spoil this prudent picture. First, the hives do not work to a fixed plan, and the populations will rise and fall in response to a number of different factors. If a colony is particularly strong, it may continue to be strong right through the autumn, especially a warm autumn, and end up using more honey than it can replenish, leaving it with no source of food when the flowers finally disappear.

Second, when the outside temperature gets below about 10°C, the bees will cluster together for warmth. This makes it difficult for them to move around the hive, and bees can starve if they're stuck on an empty comb, however much honey is stored in other parts of the hive.

So, even if we hadn't stolen the honey in the summer, a colony can still find itself short of food in winter, and it's against that possibility that we put fondant in the hive, and why we're careful to place it above the bees, where the bees are most likely to be able to get at it.

At this time of year, even the most conscientious beekeeper can find few reasons to stir themselves. Even so, every week, the Brockwell Apiary gets a brief inspection. We check if they've got enough fondant to eat and that the bees are still alive. It's a good thing to do, though dull and cold. Which is why, when anyone else is unwise enough to get within reach, we try to dress them up in bee suits and make them help. This year, we're using transparent boxes to hold the fondant, so visitors can take the roofs off and have a chance of seeing some bees without much risk of anything happening. We all pretend it is fun.

As the year draws to a close, we have had two productive seasons in a row, and we've been able to sell a respectable amount of honey. Not, perhaps, the tons of honey that the people who write the books confidently predict, but enough to impress anyone who has not got to put the stuff in jars, and that is the main thing. Competence is always an illusion, of course, but there is still some pride to be had from maintaining it.

The Honey Club

Words by Amy Lee. Photography by Charlotte Coulais

Two years ago I didn't think about bees very much, and when I did it was mostly about that fact that they hurt. My closest encounter with them had occurred when, at the age of six, I stepped on a lazy bumblebee as I ran to the swimming pool.

So how did I end up being a leader of the Honey Club, a social enterprise co-created by Wolff Olins (the brand business where I work) and charity Global Generation, with the mission to create the biggest bee-friendly community in the world?

The story begins back in 2008 with a sparse, forbidding bit of concrete on the roof of Wolff Olins' offices in King's Cross. A few passionate people in the business had decided that the roof should have a garden, and enlisted the help of Global Generation. The charity aims to show the wonders of gardening to young people growing up in King's Cross, and has expertise in enabling London-based businesses to transform their roof spaces into green oases.

The relationship grew stronger, and at the end of 2010 the charity's leader Jane Riddiford approached her friend Bethany Koby, design director at Wolff Olins, to say that Global Generation had received funding for two beehives and would the company be interested in housing some bees?

We were interested, particularly since the plight of bees is a cause that's relevant to us all. As we learned more, we realised just how important they are, both environmentally and financially. Those yellow crops you see blowing in the wind? Those hedgerows that define England's green and pleasant land? They all need bees.

We rely on bees to pollinate around a third of everything we eat, and losing them would result in a loss of billions of pounds from the UK economy. Sadly, their numbers have been rapidly declining, and it's our fault. We've introduced deadly diseases to them, and destroyed their natural feeding grounds. In the last 70 years we have cut back around 97 per cent of the grassland that used to be abundant with the wildflowers that bees love. It is therefore our responsibility to help bees thrive again.

But just as importantly, we wanted to explore how we could have a positive impact on our local community. Having been in our building on Regent's Canal for more

than 20 years, we've seen King's Cross transformed: what was once a seedy "no-go zone" is now London's next big hub for creative talent, as Central St Martins art school relocates here along with many big corporations, such as Google.

The development of the site behind St Pancras Station is changing the area beyond recognition, and Global Generation is an integral part of this progression. It is based on the site and has built temporary gardens from skips and other reclaimed building materials left over by the construction contractors. Its young volunteers, known as the Generators, all live in the area.

The next generation growing up in King's Cross needs to be given a way to become involved in the changes and opportunities that are sweeping through their backyard. It's too easy to ignore the community in the area where you work and to focus purely on where you live. But we all take a lot from the place where we spend five days out of seven, and we owe it to King's Cross to acknowledge our interdependence.

In January 2011, a bunch of us at Wolff Olins ran a workshop with the Generators. We all agreed that if we started keeping bees we didn't want it to be just a hobby or a retail venture. We wanted to create a club of engaged people who had been brought together by a common interest: learning about and helping the humble honeybee.

We wanted it to be a long-term initiative, so we would ask participants to sign up as members and pay an annual fee to attend bee-themed events that we, the founders, would run. We wanted it to be financially sustainable and so we established it as a social enterprise – an emerging type of business model in which revenue is earned and any profit is driven back into pursuing the social cause.

The Generators are aged between 14 and 19 and live on or around the edges of the King's Cross development site. They are all motivated young people, working out their role in the world, and they are key to the Honey Club's success. We hope that the enterprise will provide them with skills that will prove vital to their future.

The Generators have been involved at every stage, including co-creating the Honey Club concept, choosing the name, pitching to companies, hands-on beekeeping,

> It's too easy to ignore the community in the area where you work and to focus purely on where you live

and planning and hosting events for members. They attend regular workshops run by our team to input into how the business model should evolve, giving them the chance to learn hands-on enterprise skills and work with businesspeople on an equal basis.

This was never going to be one of those standard "corporate social responsibility" schemes, whereby companies assuage their guilt by making faceless donations or sending their employees on ad hoc away days. This was going to be a new way of bringing people together in a way that's local, active and long-term – and with bees at its heart. We now have around 100,000 bees in two hives on our roof. Our partners comprise some of the most significant members of the local business community, including the Guardian, Eurostar, Central St Martins and King's Cross property developer Argent. We have also run a series of successful apian events with themes ranging from cooking with honey to "guerrilla gardening".

We have many more initiatives on the horizon, such as an online portal for the public to access bee-based information; downloadable toolkits to enable people to set up similar bee-themed clubs; and hosting an interactive workshop with urban beekeepers to generate new beekeeping methods. So much, in fact, that this summer we welcomed Zak, a marketing undergraduate and ex-Generator, to work as a dedicated Honey Club intern – giving us direct insight into how we can create a greater impact for the young people who are involved.

It's been an incredible journey and one that is constantly evolving. For me, Yelena and Charlotte, the club's day-to-day leaders from Wolff Olins, and Stuart, our building manager (and now bee expert), it has changed our working lives: bringing us into contact with people all over London, the UK and abroad – and, most importantly, the Generators themselves.

Impact through action, not words, is key to the Honey Club's mission. Our work is all about reconnecting with the world: with the bees that keep our ecosystem living, and with the people with whom we share space every day. It's about seeing the world around us differently – a sentiment summed up by one of the Generators and trainee beekeeper, 15-year old Jihaan: "In the beginning I was really shy about working with adults because they seemed very smart and confident compared with me, and now we are on the same level. I also never imagined I would be literally working with bees. When I started I was really scared. I was always in the corner, but now the bees can be around me and I don't move. One day if I have children I know I will be able to back them up and encourage them not to be scared of insects, not to be afraid of the world."

To find out more about the Honey Club go to honeyclub.org

The best blooms for bees

Many of the prettiest flowers are also those that are best for bees. If you plan with bees in mind, you will be growing easy and beautiful plants that will look good from spring right through to winter. Bees can collect pollen and nectar from annuals, perennials, trees, herbs and fruits. The only vegetables they really like are broad and runner beans. Bees that forage on a wide range of plants are usually healthier than those that rely on a single crop, so city gardens are perfect for them. Choosing bee-friendly plants is easy; just follow the guidelines below.

Shape Honeybees have short tongues and like flowers where the pollen and nectar is easy to reach. Flat, daisy-like flowers are good, as are loose, open flowers, such as wild roses. Bees also like tubular-shaped flowers that they can get right inside. Double flowers, such as those with masses of petals, are not good because they are often highly bred and, even if they have pollen and nectar, it is almost impossible for bees to reach.

Colour Bees do not see colour in the same way that we do, but they like white, blue, purple and yellow flowers the best.

Season Bees hibernate in winter, but will wake on mild days and fly out in search of food. It is important to have some flowers in bloom from March to November.

Scent It is thought that scent is strongest when the flowers have most nectar. Any fragrant flower of the right shape will attract bees.

Wildflowers and cottage garden plants were the traditional food of bees, but it does not matter whether you plant native or exotic flowers, as long as they fit the descriptions above. Bees like tall flowers, rather than those that hug the ground, but they must be in a sheltered, sunny spot. Finally, and fairly obviously, do not use any chemicals.

Recipes

By Chloe Coker and Jane Montgomery
Food photography by Emma Mitchell

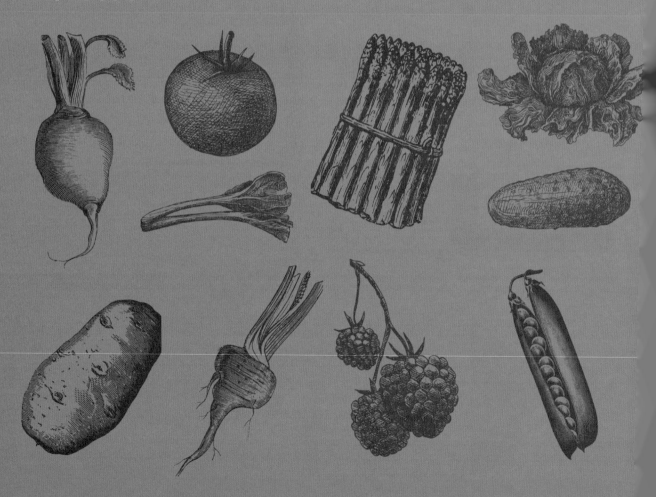

Goat's cheese, honey and walnut tart

A simple puff pastry tart is a really quick and inexpensive way to feed a crowd. Top it with whatever you have to hand – strong-flavoured cheeses work really well, while vegetables give colour and texture. It also makes a fantastic dessert: simply bake the pastry, leave it to cool, then fill it with cream or crème patissiere and top with seasonal fruit.

Serves 4 to 6
Preparation time: 25 minutes
Baking time: 10 to 15 minutes

* *300g ready-rolled puff pastry – "all butter puff" is tastiest*
* *1 egg, beaten, to glaze*
* *250g soft goat's cheese*
* *6 tbsp crème fraiche*
* *2 large eggs*
* *Zest and juice of ½ a lemon*
* *1 tbsp chopped fresh thyme, plus extra for sprinkling*
* *Salt and pepper*
* *1 apple, thinly sliced*
* *2 tbsp runny honey*
* *50g walnuts*
* *20g butter*
* *Generous pinch Maldon sea salt*

Recipe tip *leave the apple skin on for extra colour*

Preheat the oven to 200°C.

Roll out the pastry to A4 size and place it on a flat baking sheet. With a sharp knife, score a 1½ cm (¾in) border around the edge of the pastry, being careful not to cut all the way through. Pierce the centre rectangle with a fork (this will break the layers of the pastry and stop the centre rising).

Chill the pastry in the fridge until it is firm. Brush the top with a thin layer of beaten egg to glaze the pastry (be careful not to let the egg run down the edges of the pastry as this will stop it rising well). Bake in the top third of the oven for 15 minutes until well risen and golden.

While the pastry is baking, combine the goat's cheese, crème fraiche, 2 eggs, 1 tbsp lemon juice, lemon zest and fresh thyme in a bowl, then season with salt and pepper.

Cut the apple into quarters, remove the core and thinly slice.

Remove the pastry from the oven, run a sharp knife around the border, then push down the centre of the pastry where the fork marks are. Spread the goat's cheese mixture over the centre of the pastry, then arrange the apple over the top.

Place the butter and honey in a pan over a low heat and allow to dissolve. Add in the walnuts and sprinkle with a pinch of Maldon sea salt. Swirl the pan so that the nuts are well covered, then arrange them over the top of the tart. Drizzle over the honey mixture and sprinkle on some fresh thyme leaves.

Turn the oven down to 170°C and bake the tart in the centre of the oven for 10-15 minutes until the filling is set and starting to turn golden. If you prefer the tart to have a bit more colour, you can finish it under the grill.

Serving tip *sprinkle with some fresh thyme leaves and serve with a crisp green salad*

Mackerel and potato salad

This springtime salad makes the most of the seasonal flavours available – buttery new potatoes, fresh peppery watercress and crunchy spring onions. The lemon and peppered mackerel give a lovely cut through to the rich dressing, while the beetroot adds earthy sweetness and a splash of colour.

Serves 4 to 6
Preparation time: 20 minutes
Allow an extra 20 minutes to roast your own beetroot

Salad
* 600g baby new potatoes, skin intact
* 3 tbsp olive oil
* Salt and pepper
* 250g cooked beetroot (buy it cooked, but not in vinegar, or roast it yourself)
* 100g watercress
* 4 spring onions
* 300g smoked, peppered mackerel
* Handful of fresh dill, chopped, to serve

Dressing
* 200ml crème fraiche
* 100ml mayonnaise
* 1 to 2 tbsp horseradish sauce (depending on its strength)
* Zest and juice of 1 lemon
* Salt and pepper

How to roast beetroot yourself

Preheat the oven to 180°C. Cut off any leaves and wash the beetroot. Place the beetroot, skin intact, in tin foil and roast in the centre of the oven for 30 to 40 minutes until it is soft. Once cooked, you can easily peel off the skin and cut it into chunks.

Wash the baby potatoes and place them in a pan with enough boiling water to cover them. Boil on a medium-to-high heat for around 15 minutes, until a knife will go through the centre. Drain well, transfer to a bowl and stir through the olive oil. Leave to cool slightly.

Wash and drain the watercress, remove any woody stalks and break into bite-size pieces. Slice the spring onions and flake the smoked mackerel into large chunks.

To make the dressing, combine the crème fraiche, mayonnaise and horseradish sauce. Stir through the lemon zest and 1 tbsp of lemon juice. Season with salt and pepper. Taste the dressing and adjust with further lemon juice or horseradish to your taste.

Stir the dressing through the potatoes. Then stir in the watercress, spring onions, mackerel and a handful of chopped dill. Finally, gently stir through the pieces of beetroot until just combined (be careful not to stir it too much or it will turn the salad pink). Finish with a sprinkling of fresh dill and some freshly ground black pepper.

Tomato tatin

make in summer

A savoury tatin is a fantastic way to serve and showcase seasonal vegetables. Tomatoes make a tasty and colourful summer tatin, but can easily be exchanged for whatever is in season such as chicory, shallots or peppers. Just make sure the vegetables are almost cooked and caramelised before the pastry goes on. Once it is cooked, you can top it with fresh herbs and crumbled cheese for extra colour and flavour.

Serves 4 to 6
Preparation time: 20 minutes
Cooking time: 10 to 15 minutes

Pastry
* 90g cold butter
* 160g plain flour
* 35g parmesan cheese, finely grated
* 1 tsp dried mixed herbs
* 1 egg yolk
* 2 tbsp water

Filling
* 2 red onions, finely sliced
* 25g butter
* 2 tbsp olive oil
* 2 tsp brown sugar
* 1 tbsp water
* 1 tbsp honey
* 1 tsp balsamic vinegar
* 1 garlic clove, crushed
* Chopped fresh rosemary
* 400g baby plum or cherry tomatoes

Optional
* ½ fresh chilli, finely diced
* 2 tbsp white wine
* Feta and rosemary to top

Recipe tip *use little meli melo tomatoes for a mix of colour*

Serving tip *sprinkle with some crumbled feta and chopped fresh rosemary*

Preheat the oven to 180°C. You will need an oven-proof frying pan. We used a 20cm (8in) cast-iron pan.

To make the pastry: keep the butter in the fridge until you are ready to use it. Chop the butter into cubes, then rub it into the flour until it is the consistency of fine breadcrumbs (using a food processor makes light work of this). Stir through the grated parmesan and dried mixed herbs. In a separate small bowl, mix the egg yolk with 2 tbsp water until well combined. Place 2 tbsp of the egg mixture into the flour and combine with a knife until it forms large flakes. Put your hand in the bowl and bring the pastry together. If the pastry is very dry and crumbly, add a little more of the egg mixture.

Roll the pastry into a circle the size of the frying pan and about ½cm (¾in) thick. Chill in the fridge until you are ready to use it.

Place the red onions in the frying pan with the butter, 1 tbsp olive oil, 1 tbsp water and 2 tsp brown sugar. Cook on a low heat for about 8 minutes until they soften but don't take on any colour.

When the onions are cooked, remove them from the pan and set aside. Using the same pan, add in 1 tbsp olive oil, 1 tbsp honey and 1 tsp balsamic vinegar. Put the pan over a medium heat and stir until the honey has dissolved and the mixture bubbles. Add in the crushed garlic, chopped fresh rosemary and chilli and cook for 2 minutes.

Cover the base of the pan with the tomatoes, then pour over 2 tbsp white wine or water. Cook over a medium heat for 5 minutes until the tomatoes soften slightly but still hold their shape. Lay the cooked red onions on top of the tomatoes, using them to fill any gaps.

Finally, lay the pastry over the top and push the edges down into the edges of the frying pan so that it is well sealed. Transfer the pan to the top shelf of the oven and cook for 15-20 minutes until the pastry is cooked and golden.

Remove the frying pan from the oven and leave to cool slightly for a minute or two. Run a knife around the edge of the pan to release the tart, then place a serving dish over the top of the frying pan and carefully flip it over.

make in summer

Raspberry scones

Raspberries give a sharp fruity twist to the traditional scone. You can use any seasonal berries that you have to hand – try blueberries, blackberries or cranberries, or any dried fruit works well. If you are using fresh berries, make sure they are firm – don't use frozen berries, as they are too soft.

Makes 8
Preparation time: 15 minutes
Baking time: 15 to 20 minutes

* *300g plain flour*
* *2 tsp baking powder*
* *90g butter*
* *50g golden caster sugar*
* *100ml buttermilk*
* *1 tsp good-quality vanilla extract*
* *80g fresh berries or 50g dried berries*
* *2 tbsp milk and 1 tbsp golden caster sugar to glaze*
* *Circular cutter*
* *Jam and clotted cream to serve*

Recipe tip *if you don't have buttermilk, just add a tablespoon of lemon juice to milk and leave it for a minute or two before use*

Serving tip *slather with some jam and indulgent clotted cream*

Preheat the oven to 180°C and flour a baking sheet.

Sieve together the flour and baking powder. Keep the butter in the fridge until you are ready to use it. Cut it into cubes, then rub it into the flour with your fingertips until it reaches the consistency of breadcrumbs. If you have a food processor, use it to rub in the butter by gently pulsing the mixture until it has a breadcrumb texture.

Stir through the sugar.

Stir the buttermilk (or lemon and milk mixture) through the flour mixture, until it forms large flakes. At this point, carefully stir through the berries, then bring the mixture together with your hands to form a dough. The dough will be quite wet and sticky from the berries.

Flour your hands and generously flour the work surface, then pat down the dough to 4cm (1½in) thickness (do not roll it out). Using a cutter, cut out the scones and transfer them to the baking sheet. Scrunch together any leftover mixture with your hands and cut out more scones until you have used up all of the mixture.

In a cup, combine 2 tbsp milk with 1 tbsp golden caster sugar. Using a pastry brush, brush the top of the scones with the milk mixture, taking care not to let it run down the sides of the scones.

Bake the scones in the top third of the oven for around 15-20 minutes, until they are firm and golden. Cool on a wire rack.

Date slice

make
in
autumn

This slice is great for a picnic or for a hearty snack on a long walk. It works really well with different flavoured fillings, from mincemeat or apple purée, to jam or chocolate chunks. Simply use whatever you have in the cupboard, or is in season.

Makes 12 to 16 portions
Preparation time: 25 minutes
Baking time: 20 to 25 minutes

Date paste
* *250g dates*
* *150ml water*
* *Zest of ½ a lemon*
* *1 tsp good-quality vanilla extract*

Oat slice
* *225g butter*
* *150g light brown sugar*
* *3 tbsp honey*
* *250g wholemeal, plain or gluten-free flour, sifted*
* *250g rolled oats*

Optional
* *2 tsp mixed spice*

 Recipe tip *you could replace 100g of the rolled oats with chopped nuts*

Preheat the oven to 170°C.

Grease a brownie tin or small roasting tray and line it with non-stick baking paper. We used a 20cm (8in) square tin.

Place all the ingredients in a pan and simmer until the dates break down and start to form a purée. Crush any large pieces with a spoon, or blitz in a food processor if you prefer a smooth paste.

Place the butter, sugar and honey in a pan over a low-to-medium heat and stir gently until the butter has melted and the sugar and honey have dissolved.

In a bowl, mix together the flour, oats and mixed spice, then stir through the butter mixture until it is well combined.

Place half of the mixture in the base of the lined tin. Then dollop the date purée onto the corners and centre, and smooth into an even layer.

Spoon the rest of the oat mixture on top and press down so that it forms a firm layer.

Bake in the top third of the oven until the oats are golden (about 20-25 minutes). Roughly cut into squares while it is still warm in the tin, then leave to cool.

Pork, apple and black pudding pasties

These pasties are perfect for an autumn picnic. Buy some good-quality pork sausages or roast a shoulder of pork and use up the leftovers. If you are short of time, serve the filling in some crusty rolls with horseradish or apple sauce - great for a bonfire night snack with friends.

Makes 6 to 8 (depending on size)
Preparation time: 20 minutes
Chill pasties for 20 minutes (or ahead of time), before baking for 20 minutes

Pastry
* 375g plain flour
* ¼ tsp salt
* 170g butter
* 1 egg
* 90ml chilled water
* 1 egg, beaten, to glaze

Optional
* Dried herbs
* Seeds to sprinkle on top

Filling
* 400g good-quality pork sausages or 200g roast pork
* 5 shallots, roasted, then separated
* 180g black pudding
* 3 tbsp chunky apple sauce
* 1 tsp wholegrain mustard
* 50ml cider
* 1 tbsp chopped fresh thyme
* Salt and pepper

Sift the flour and salt together. Then rub in the butter with your fingertips or, alternatively, pulse the flour, salt and butter in a food processor until it looks like breadcrumbs.

Add the egg and ¾ of the water and stir until the pastry comes together to form a soft, but not wet, dough. Add more water if required to bring it together.

Sprinkle a little flour on the work surface, shape the dough into a flat puck, wrap it in cling film and chill for around 15 minutes.

Preheat the oven to 180°C. Cut the shallots in half and roast them in the oven with the sausages and black pudding for 20 minutes. Cut the sausages into pieces, crumble the black pudding and pull apart the roasted onions. If you are using roast pork, roast the shallots and black pudding as above and cut the pork into bite-size pieces. Combine in a bowl with the remaining filling ingredients and season well with salt and pepper.

On a lightly floured surface, roll out the pastry to ½cm (¼in) thickness, then cut out circles of 10-15cm (4-6in) in diameter using a template (a side plate works well) or pastry cutter.

Place 2 tbsp of the filling slightly off-centre, allowing a ½cm (¼in) gap to the edge. Wet the edge with a little water, fold over the pastry in half, and seal with gentle pressure, using the blunt side of a cutlery knife to indent around the edges.

Place on a baking sheet, lightly glaze with beaten egg and sprinkle with seeds. Chill in the fridge until the pastry is firm to touch (about 20 minutes). You can make the pasties ahead, wrap them and freeze them or keep them in the fridge at this stage.

Cook for 20 minutes, or until light golden brown.

Damson gin

make in autumn

Damson gin is a fantastically indulgent winter warmer. Serve as an after-dinner drink with an ice cube, or use as a base for a simple champagne cocktail. A splash of damson gin is also a great addition to sauces for strong-flavoured meats such as duck and venison.

Preparation time: 3 months!

* 1lb damson plums
* 225g caster sugar (or granulated)
* 1 litre good-quality neutral gin

Optional
* 2 tsp vanilla extract

Recipe tip *save some of the strained fruit and freeze to use as flavoursome ice cubes or to give flavour to stews.*

Technically, the gin can be drunk from 3 months, but the flavour does improve over time if you can hold out. Also if you can keep a couple of bottles back you can start to compare vintages year on year.

If you have time, prick each damson a few times with a pin. Alternatively, freeze the damsons for a few days before making the gin; this will help to break the skins and start to break down the cells of the fruit.

Weigh the ingredients.

Wash the damsons, removing leaves and stalks.

If you have the time, prick each damson a few times with a pin.

Mix the damsons with the sugar and half-fill an appropriate storage jar or bottle – usually glass with a lid or cork stopper. Old spirit bottles work well. Then fill up the jar or bottle with the gin.

Store in a cool dark environment.

Turn or shake the bottle every day if you remember.

After three months, strain the gin through a sieve and muslin.

Decant into your preferred drinking vessels to store, drink or give as presents.

Note on sterilising

Bottles used for making and storing the gin must be sterilised first. To sterilise, wash bottles well in soapy water and then place in a low oven – less than 100°C – for a few minutes until hot. Alternatively, place in a hot dishwasher cycle (70°C), which will also ensure the bottles are sterilised. Ensure there are no plastic elements on the bottles and ensure all lids are off when sterilising.

make in winter

Roast cauliflower and almond soup

Turn the humble cauliflower into a lovely velvety soup with this quick and simple recipe. Pack it into a flask to warm you through on a cold day out or enjoy it with some crusty bread by the fire when you get home.

Serves 4
Preparation time: 35 minutes
(includes 15 minutes to simmer)

* 1 medium cauliflower
* 2 garlic cloves, skin intact
* 3 tbsp olive oil
* 4 tbsp ground almonds
* 1 white onion, diced
* 1 white potato (about 200g),
  peeled and cut into 2cm (¾in) chunks
* 500ml vegetable stock
* 3 tbsp single cream
* Grated nutmeg
* Salt and pepper

Serving tip *serve with a drizzle of extra-virgin olive oil, some toasted almonds or some fresh thyme leaves*

Preheat the oven to 170°C. Chop the cauliflower into large pieces and put it in a roasting tin with the garlic cloves. Drizzle with 2 tbsp olive oil and season with salt and pepper. Roast in the centre of the oven for 15 minutes until the cauliflower starts to soften and turn golden. Sprinkle over the ground almonds and roast for a further 5 minutes.

Meanwhile, dice the onion and place it in a large saucepan with 1 tbsp olive oil and 1 tbsp water. Gently cook over a low heat for about 8 minutes until the onion has softened but not taken on any colour. Add the potato and stir until it is covered in the oil and onion, then add in the roasted cauliflower and almonds. Squeeze out the garlic cloves from their skins, crush them with a fork and add them to the pan. Pour over 500ml vegetable stock and bring to the boil. Simmer for about 15 minutes until the potato and cauliflower are nice and soft.

Blitz the soup with a hand blender or liquidiser. For a really smooth soup you can pass it through a sieve.

Finally, stir through the cream and season to taste with salt, pepper and grated nutmeg.

Potted duck

This is two recipes in one: first you make a gorgeous confit duck – perfect for eating shredded in a salad or hot with some sauté potatoes; then you can make it into a pâté, ideal for a picnic or to serve as a canapé. If you don't have time to confit your duck legs, you can buy confit duck in good supermarkets and delis.

Serves 4 to 8
Preparation time: 5 to 10 minutes
Marinating time: at least 2 hours
Cooking time: 3 hours

For the confit duck
* *4 duck legs (about 900g)*
* *4 cloves garlic*
* *2 sprigs fresh rosemary*
* *4 sprigs fresh thyme*
* *Ground black pepper*
* *1½ tbsp sea salt*
* *300g goose or duck fat, or olive oil*

Marinate the duck legs: Peel and slice 1 clove of garlic and mix it together with a sprig of rosemary (torn into pieces), 2 sprigs of fresh thyme, some ground black pepper and 1½ tbsp sea salt. Make holes in the skin of the duck legs with a sharp knife and rub in marinade. Place the duck legs skin side down in a dish, wrap with cling film and leave to marinate in the fridge for at least 2 hours or overnight if possible.

Confit the duck legs: preheat the oven to 150°C. Wipe off the marinade with a paper towel. Place the duck legs skin side down in an oven-proof dish that is just big enough to hold them so that they fit snugly on the bottom. Cut the remaining garlic cloves into pieces and dot them around the dish with the remaining rosemary and thyme. Melt the goose or duck fat if you are using it (alternatively you can use olive oil), then pour it over the duck legs until they are well covered – they should be almost submerged. You can top up the fat with some olive oil if you don't have quite enough. Cover with a lid and cook in the centre of the oven for 3 hours until the meat is falling off the bones.

To store the confit: place the duck legs in a clean, preferably airtight container, then strain the fat and pour it over them so that they are totally submerged, sealing them. They can be stored in the fridge like this for a few weeks.

To use the duck legs, wipe off the fat. You can shred the duck legs into a salad or, to crisp up the skin, preheat the oven to 190°C. Place the duck legs skin side up on a rack in a roasting tin and roast in the top third of the oven for about 15 minutes until they are warm through and the skin is crisp. Serve with sauté potatoes cooked in a bit of the duck fat or some flageolet beans.

Preparation time: 10 to 15 minutes

For the potted duck
* *4 confit duck legs*
* *Zest and juice of ½ a lemon*
* *2 tbsp fat from cooking the duck, melted, plus extra for sealing*
* *Handful fresh parsley, finely chopped*
* *2 sprigs fresh thyme, finely chopped*
* *Salt and pepper*

Optional
* *2 tbsp cognac*
* *Half a shallot, very finely diced*

Wash the jars or pots you plan to use in hot soapy water, then fill them with boiling water or put them in the oven at about 100°C to sterilise them.

Wipe the fat off the duck legs, then shred them into a bowl. Stir through the lemon zest and juice, cognac and duck fat. For a coarse pâté, use a fork to break down the meat into fine shreds. For a smoother pâté, you can blitz the mixture in a food processor on a pulse – do this carefully as you do not want it to turn to mush.

Stir through the freshly chopped herbs, and shallot if you are using it, and season well with salt and pepper. Taste and adjust the seasoning with extra lemon juice and cognac.

Press the mixture tightly into your jars. If you are not using the pâté straight away, melt some duck fat and pour it into the top of the jar or pot to form a seal. This will keep in the fridge for a couple of days. If you are keeping the potted duck, confit the duck legs fresh – do not use ones that have already been in the fridge for a few weeks.

Serving tip *serve with toast, red onion chutney, capers and cornichons*

Acknowledgements

We would like to thank the following people and organisations for their help during the creation of this book: Nick Bertrand, Mark Spencer, Mathew Frith, the London Biodiversity Partnership, the Ruislip Woods Trust, Theo Pike, Peter O' Hare, London Orchard Project, Friends of the Great North Wood, Sara Ward, Brockwell Park Community Greenhouses, Hackney City Farm, Andy Willmore and Alex Robb of London Wildlife Trust, and the London Transport Museum.

This book and magazine would not be here without the hard work and support of our contributors and friends. In particular we would like to thank our parents and siblings, Patrick Dalton, Amy Wicks, Lee Hickman, Natalie Mosquera, Edward Felton, Jennifer Rigby, Ellie Tennant, Tom Hartford, Lynne Scott, Giles Barrie, Richard Krzyzak, Andrew Diprose, Sheli Rodney, Felicity Kent, Andrea Carpenter, Helen Babbs, Rachel Warne, Jon Cardwell, Silvana De Soissons, Leila Odish, Liz Hague, Hannah O'Shea, Chris O'Shea, Martha Sims, Rory Brady, Anne-Marie Young, Alison Hargreaves, Katherine George, Jo Bailey, James Tout, Vidisha Gaglani, Mat McNerney, Kerry Flynn, Matt Flynn, Rose Phillips, Sam Rogers, Laura Woolf, Tom Blanks, Jack McGinity, Giles Hill, Kate Hill, Helen Kichenbrand, Cliff Phillips, Rhona Sleator, Giada Farina, Emily Hope, Rhiannon Larkman, Claer Barrett, Bing Hobson, Jess Palmer, Leo Twiddy, Christopher Woodward, Carlie Hoare, Lucy Shuter-Givry, Geoffroy Givry, Emma Hogwood, Lynne Miles, Nicky Forster, Joanne McAlroy, Neil Weatherall, Natalie Thorn, Hazel Nicholls, Helen Ginn, Matt Brown and the *Londonist*, Jeremy Leslie and Anthony Peters.

Most of all we would like to thank our long-suffering husbands Sam Hobson and Mike Phillips, and Daniel Blackburn for his support during the compilation of this book and the magazine.

Production

Daniel Blackburn, Sheli Rodney and Felicity Kent

Retouching by Sam Twiddy

About the authors

Lucy Scott and Tina Smith created *Lost in London* magazine in the autumn of 2010. It was intended to be a one-off portfolio project, written and designed for city-dwellers seeking a simpler life. It has since gone on to be one of the foremost independent magazine titles around.

This is their first book.

Contributors

 Jon Cardwell is a London-based photographer who loves the green spaces of the city and beyond. *joncardwell.com*

 Helen Babbs is a writer and wild London explorer. She posts her work at *helenbabbs.wordpress.com* and shares her roof garden adventures at *aerialediblegardening.co.uk*

 Daisy Hardman lives in west London and is an illustrator with a passion for materials, textures and mark-making. She is inspired by nature and peculiar people. *daisyhardmanillustration.tumblr.com*

 Lee Hickman is a retoucher, photographer and beard wearer, when his girlfriend lets him get away with it. *leetotheretouch@gmail.com*

 Tom Bingham is an illustrator based in the north of England. He puts pencil to paper and takes inspiration from the things he loves around him: food, nature and friendly faces.

 Rachel Warne is a lover of the outdoors and all things green. She likes to get up with the larks and photograph gardens. *rae@rachelwarne.co.uk*

 Sam Hobson is a freelance photographer specialising in urban wildlife, conservation and the environment. *Sam@samhobson.co.uk*

 Karolin Schnoor is a German designer and illustrator working in south London. *karolinschnoor.co.uk*

 Penny Greenhough is a single mother who lives in Peckham with her two daughters. She's an urban shrub-rummaging pioneer who harvests wild food from the streets of south-east London.

 Mark James Pearson is a natural history writer and conservationist, specialising in birds; he also makes music as Morning Bride. His work is collected at *markjamespearson.wordpress.com*

 Bertie Gregory has a passion for wildlife and wildlife photography. He is one of 20 young photographers on the 2020VISION project. *bertiegregoryphotography.com*

Adam Johann Lang is a photographer who aspires to have a big enough London garden to keep alpacas. *adamjohannlang.co.uk, adamjohannlang@blueyonder.co.uk*

 Grace Lee is a Tokyo-based illustrator who seeks out pockets of calm in city life. She loves to draw inanimate objects, animals with masks and things her mum likes. *behance.net/gracelee*

 Victoria Nightingale uses reportage and portraiture to tell a story. Her work has featured in *The Sunday Times, Country Life* and *The Face*. *victorianightingale.co.uk*

 Natalie Mosquera's background is in graphic design for magazines and fashion brands, but her true creative enthusiasm lies in hand-drawn illustration. *natalie@natalieboo.com*

 Ben Quinton studied commercial photography at the Arts University College Bournemouth. He likes large mugs of coffee, exploring, and annoying friends with his persistent picture-taking. *benquinton.co.uk*

 Alice Potter is a designer and illustrator living and working in London. Big colours, strong shapes and unforgiving lines continuously creep into her work. *alicepotter.co.uk*

 Patrick Dalton is a photographer who spends his time documenting the uglier and weirder sides of London for *shitlondon.co.uk*. Despite its title, he loves the place... mostly. *shhhlondon@gmail.com*

 Keiran Perry is a photographer specialising in portraiture. He loves climbing, photography, the great outdoors and, most of all, combining all three. *keiranperry1@gmail.com*

 Joe McGorty is a photographer interested in people and stories that show the quirkier side of life. *joemcgorty.com, info@joemcgorty.com*

 Ellie Tennant is a London-based freelance interiors journalist, blogger and stylist. She specialises in trends, interviews, shopping, features and design. *ellietennant.com*

 Amy Lee works for Wolff Olins, where she co-founded The Honey Club: a social enterprise that aims to build the biggest bee-friendly community in the world. *honeyclub.org*

Laurie Tuffrey is a freelance writer who grew up in the Peak District. He is currently based in south London, writing about music, nature and the environment. *laurietuffrey@gmail.com*

 Jojo Tulloh lives in east London with her husband, three daughters and a large black cat. She is the food editor of *The Week* magazine. *jojotulloh.com*

 Christopher Stocks is a writer and editor who lives in Bloomsbury. His social history of British fruit and vegetables, *Forgotten Fruits*, is published by Windmill Books. *christopherstocks.com*

 Edward Felton is a photographer, naturalist and conservationist. He is fascinated by the drama and complexity of the natural world. *edwardfelton.co.uk*

 Clementine Mitchell has created illustration and design since graduating from Central Saint Martins. She utilises a range of media including printmaking, animation and drawing. *clementinemitchell@yahoo.co.uk*

 Jane McMorland Hunter writes books on the good things in life: gardening, needlecraft, cookery, orchards and the pleasures of living in London. *foxedbooks.com*

 John Andrews deals in Vintage Fishing Tackle for the Soul on Thursdays, 8am-3pm, at Spitalfields market. He writes for publications including *Caught by the River*. *andrewsofarcadiascrapbook.blogspot.com*

 Judy Lumley's work is primarily focused on printmaking, where she uses lino to explore the interplay of pattern, texture and colour. *judylumley.com*

 Emma Block's illustration is inspired by the people she meets in her everyday life, old photos, vintage clothes, travel, 1950s illustration and 1930s jazz. *emmablock.co.uk*

 Sue Gent uses screenprint, linocut and watercolour throughout her work. She is inspired by many things - among them mythology, folklore and the natural world. *lupercaliadesign.com*

 Micha Theiner is a freelance photographer working in London, specialising in portraits, features and issue-based documentary projects. *michatheiner.com*

Chloe Coker is a freelance chef and cookery teacher. She makes bespoke wedding cakes and runs the personal cheffing company CityCook. *chloecoker.com, citycook.co.uk*

Richard Jones is an entomologist and writer. As well as carrying out ecological surveys he has recently published *Extreme Insects*, *Mosquito* and *The Little Book of Nits*. *bugmanjones.com*

Tom Hartford is a photographer who grew up in rural Lincolnshire. He now lives and works in London. *tomhartford.co.uk, tom@tomhartford.co.uk*

Jane Montgomery is a personal chef and cookery teacher. She runs CityCook, which specialises in bespoke cheffing and cookery lessons for busy people. *citycook.co.uk*

Emma Mitchell lives with her husband and two children in Northamptonshire. She has been a photographer for over ten years, and loves London to work, shop and find inspiring ideas. *emmamitchell.co.uk*

Camila Ruz is a science journalist living in west London. Trained as a zoologist, she writes about creatures great and small. *camilaruz.wordpress.com*

Simon Wilks is a volunteer at Brockwell Park Community Garden Greenhouses. His journal on beekeeping can be found at *brockwellgreenhouses.org.uk*

Amie Jones is a London-based designer and illustrator with a love of colour and pattern. *amieracheljones@gmail.com*

Ciara Phelan is a freelance illustrator working from OPEN Studio in north London. She enjoys collecting vintage things and cutting stuff out of paper. *hello@iamciara.co.uk*

Amy Wicks has a passion for craft within design. She has designed for Habitat, Paperchase, Oasis and Warehouse. *amywicks@gmail.com*

First published in the United Kingdom in 2013 by
Portico, 10 Southcombe Street, London W14 0RA

An imprint of Anova Books Company Ltd

ISBN 978-190755-460-5

A CIP catalogue for this book is available from the British Library.

10 9 8 7 6 5 4 3 2 1

Advisory Note
The methods and activities described herein have been used by the subjects but by no means represent authoritative or definitive guidance. Reasonable care has been taken to ensure the accuracy of the information and processes described herein however it is for general interest and in no way replaces professional advice as to the relative safety of carrying out the activities or eating wild plants, fungi and other wild foods. Neither the authors nor the publishers make any warranties as to the safety or legality of carrying out the activities described or the consumption of any wild foods. This book is sold on the understanding that the publishers and the authors cannot accept any responsibility for any accident incurred or damage suffered as result of following any of the suggestions contained herein and any liability for inaccuracies or errors relating to the material contained in the book is expressly excluded to the fullest extent permitted by law.

Reproduction by Mission Productions Ltd, Hong Kong
Printed and bound by 1010 Printing International Ltd, China

This book can be ordered direct from the publisher at www.anova.books.com

The end

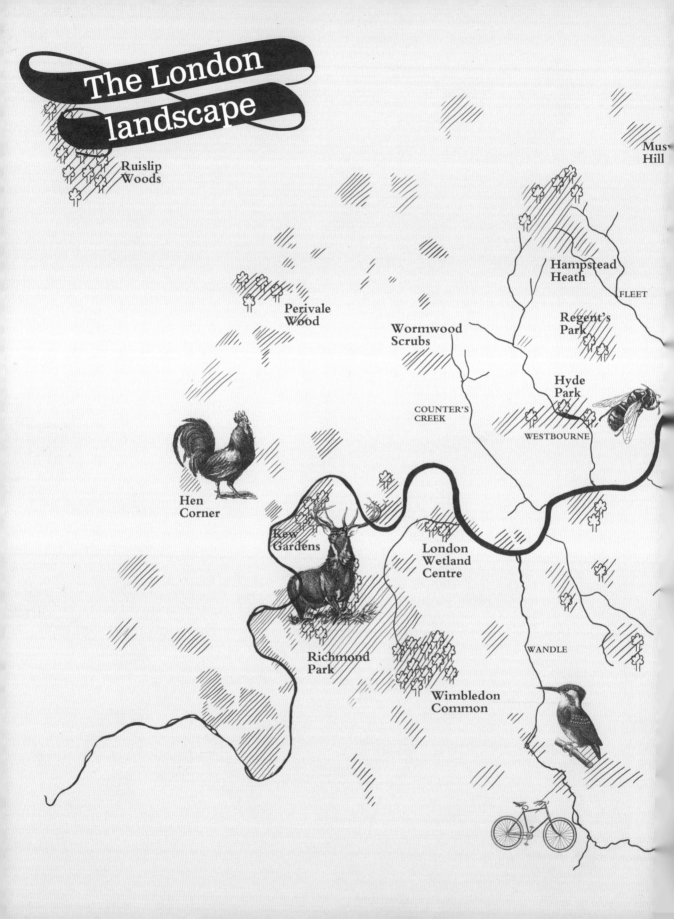

The London landscape

Ruislip
Woods

Mus<
Hill

Hampstead
Heath

FLEET

Perivale
Wood

Wormwood
Scrubs

Regent's
Park

Hyde
Park

COUNTER'S
CREEK

WESTBOURNE

Hen
Corner

Kew
Gardens

London
Wetland
Centre

Richmond
Park

WANDLE

Wimbledon
Common